THE NATIONAL COMMISSION ON FISCAL RESPONSIBILITY AND REFORM

The Moment of Truth

DECEMBER 2010

The Moment of Truth

REPORT OF THE NATIONAL COMMISSION ON FISCAL RESPONSIBILITY AND REFORM

December 2010

The Moment of Truth: Report of the National Commission on Fiscal Responsibility and Reform

Table of Contents

Tables and Figures

Preamble

Throughout our nation's history, Americans have found the courage to do right by our children's future. Deep down, every American knows we face a moment of truth once again. We cannot play games or put off hard choices any longer. Without regard to party, we have a patriotic duty to keep the promise of America to give our children and grandchildren a better life.

Our challenge is clear and inescapable: America cannot be great if we go broke. Our businesses will not be able to grow and create jobs, and our workers will not be able to compete successfully for the jobs of the future without a plan to get this crushing debt burden off our backs.

Ever since the economic downturn, families across the country have huddled around kitchen tables, making tough choices about what they hold most dear and what they can learn to live without. They expect and deserve their leaders to do the same. The American people are counting on us to put politics aside, pull together not pull apart, and agree on a plan to live within our means and make America strong for the long haul.

As members of the National Commission on Fiscal Responsibility and Reform, we spent the past eight months studying the same cold, hard facts. Together, we have reached these unavoidable conclusions: The problem is real. The solution will be painful. There is no easy way out. Everything must be on the table. And Washington <u>must</u> lead.

We come from different backgrounds, represent different regions, and belong to different parties, but we share a common belief that America's long-term fiscal gap is unsustainable and, if left unchecked, will see our children and grandchildren living in a poorer, weaker nation. In the words of Senator Tom Coburn, "We keep kicking the can down the road, and splashing the soup all over our grandchildren." Every modest sacrifice we refuse to make today only forces far greater sacrifices of hope and opportunity upon the next generation.

Over the course of our deliberations, the urgency of our mission has become all the more apparent. The contagion of debt that began in Greece and continues to sweep through Europe shows us clearly that no economy will be immune. If the U.S. does not put its house in order, the reckoning will be sure and the devastation severe.

The President and the leaders of both parties in both chambers of Congress asked us to address the nation's fiscal challenges in this decade and beyond. We have worked to offer an aggressive, fair, balanced, and bipartisan proposal – a proposal as serious as the problems we face. None of us likes every element of our plan, and each of us had to tolerate provisions we previously or presently oppose in order to reach a principled compromise. We were willing to put our differences aside to forge a plan because our nation will certainly be lost without one.

We do not pretend to have all the answers. We offer our plan as the starting point for a serious national conversation in which every citizen has an interest and all should have a say. Our leaders have a responsibility to level with Americans about the choices we face, and to enlist the ingenuity and determination of the American people in rising to the challenge.

We believe neither party can fix this problem on its own, and both parties have a responsibility to do their part. The American people are a long way ahead of the political system in recognizing that now is the time to act. We believe that far from penalizing their leaders for making the tough choices, Americans will punish politicians for backing down – and well they should.

In the weeks and months to come, countless advocacy groups and special interests will try mightily through expensive, dramatic, and heart-wrenching media assaults to exempt themselves from shared sacrifice and common purpose. The national interest, not special interests, must prevail. We urge leaders and citizens with principled concerns about any of our recommendations to follow what we call the Becerra Rule: Don't shoot down an idea without offering a better idea in its place.

After all the talk about debt and deficits, it is long past time for America's leaders to put up or shut up. The era of debt denial is over, and there can be no turning back. We sign our names to this plan because we love our children, our grandchildren, and our country too much not to act while we still have the chance to secure a better future for all our fellow citizens.

The Mission

Figure 1: Debt as a Percent of GDP

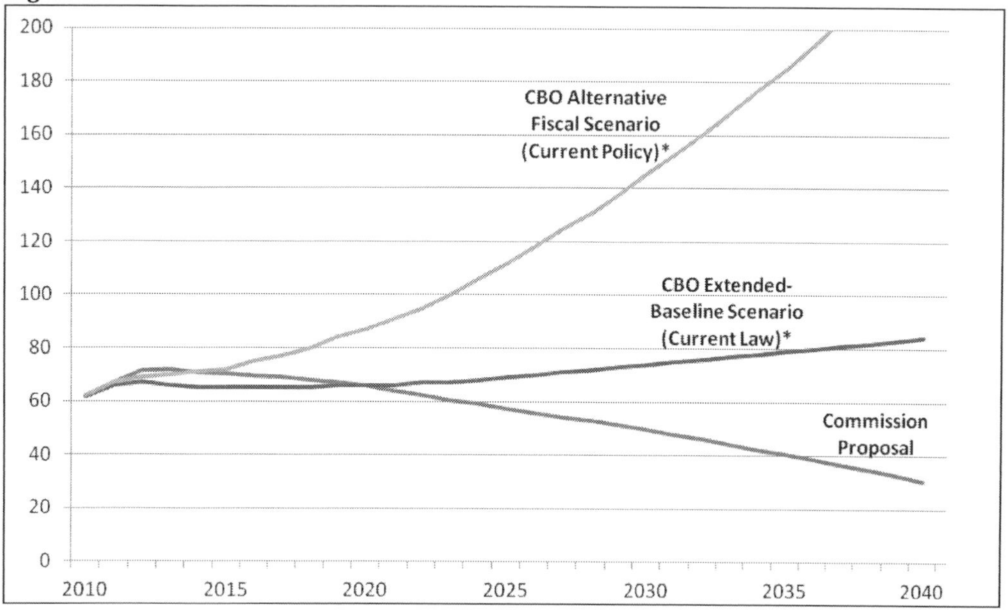

The Extended-Baseline Scenario generally assumes continuation of current law. The Alternative Fiscal Scenario incorporates several changes to current law considered likely to happen, including the renewal of the 2001/2003 tax cuts on income below $250,000 per year, continued Alternative Minimum Tax (AMT) patches, the continuation of the estate tax at 2009 levels, and continued Medicare "Doc Fixes." The Alternative Fiscal Scenario also assumes discretionary spending grows with Gross Domestic Product (GDP) rather than to inflation over the next decade, that revenue does not increase as a percent of GDP after 2020, and that certain cost-reducing measures in the health reform legislation are unsuccessful in slowing cost growth after 2020.

The Looming Fiscal Crisis

Our nation is on an unsustainable fiscal path. Spending is rising and revenues are falling short, requiring the government to borrow huge sums each year to make up the difference. We face staggering deficits. In 2010, federal spending was nearly 24 percent of Gross Domestic Product (GDP), the value of all goods and services produced in the economy. Only during World War II was federal spending a larger part of the economy. Tax revenues stood at 15 percent of GDP this year, the lowest level since 1950. The gap between spending and revenue – the budget deficit – was just under nine percent of GDP.

Since the last time our budget was balanced in 2001, the federal debt has increased dramatically, rising from 33 percent of GDP to 62 percent of GDP in 2010. The escalation was driven in large part by two wars and a slew of fiscally irresponsible policies, along with a deep economic downturn. We have arrived at the moment of truth, and neither political party is without blame.

Economic recovery will improve the deficit situation in the short run because revenues will rise as people go back to work, and money spent on the social safety net will decline as fewer people are forced to rely on it. But even after the economy recovers, federal spending is projected to increase faster than revenues, so the government will have to continue borrowing money to spend. The Congressional Budget Office (CBO) projects if we continue on our current course, deficits will remain high throughout the rest of this decade and beyond, and debt will spiral ever higher, reaching 90 percent of GDP in 2020.

Over the long run, as the baby boomers retire and health care costs continue to grow, the situation will become far worse. By 2025 revenue will be able to finance only interest payments, Medicare, Medicaid, and Social Security. Every other federal government activity – from national defense and homeland security to transportation and energy – will have to be paid for with borrowed money. Debt held by the public will outstrip the entire American economy, growing to as much as 185 percent of GDP by 2035. Interest on the debt could rise to nearly $1 trillion by 2020. These mandatory payments – which buy absolutely no goods or services – will squeeze out funding for all other priorities.

Federal debt this high is unsustainable. It will drive up interest rates for all borrowers – businesses and individuals – and curtail economic growth by crowding out private investment. By making it more expensive for entrepreneurs and businesses to raise capital, innovate, and create jobs, rising debt could reduce per-capita GDP, each American's share of the nation's economy, by as much as 15 percent by 2035.

Rising debt will also hamstring the government, depriving it of the resources needed to respond to future crises and invest in other priorities. Deficit spending is often used to respond to short-term financial "emergency" needs such as wars or recessions. If our national debt grows higher, the federal government may even have difficulty borrowing funds at an affordable interest rate, preventing it from effectively responding.

Large debt will put America at risk by exposing it to foreign creditors. They currently own more than half our public debt, and the interest we pay them reduces our own standard of living. The single largest foreign holder of our debt is China, a nation that may not share our country's aspirations and strategic interests. In a worst-case scenario, investors could lose confidence that our nation is able or willing to repay its loans – possibly triggering a debt crisis that would force the government to implement the most stringent of austerity measures.

Predicting the precise level of public debt that would trigger such a crisis is difficult, but a key factor may be whether the debt has been stabilized as a share of the economy or if it continues to rise. Investors, reluctant to risk throwing good money after bad, are sure to be far more concerned about rising debt than stable debt. In a recent briefing on the risk of a fiscal crisis, CBO explained that while "there is no identifiable tipping point of debt relative to GDP indicating that a crisis is likely or imminent," the U.S. debt-to-GDP ratio is "climbing into unfamiliar territory" and "the higher the debt, the greater the risk of such a crisis."[1]

If we do not act soon to reassure the markets, the risk of a crisis will increase, and the options available to avert or remedy the crisis will both narrow and become more stringent. If we wait ten years, CBO projects our economy could shrink by as much as 2 percent, and spending cuts and tax increases needed to plug the hole could nearly double what is needed today. Continued inaction is not a viable option, and not an acceptable course for a responsible government.

---

[1] CBO, *Federal Debt and the Risk of a Fiscal Crisis* (July 2010).

Our Guiding Principles and Values

In establishing this Commission, the President gave us a two-part mission: to bring the budget into primary balance (balance excluding interest costs) in 2015, and to meaningfully improve the long-run fiscal outlook. Our recommendations accomplish both of these goals, while keeping the following core principles in mind:

We all have a patriotic duty to make America better off tomorrow than it is today. Americans are counting on us to pull together, not pull apart, to put politics aside and do the right thing for future generations. Our country's economic and national security depend on us putting our fiscal house in order.

Don't disrupt the fragile economic recovery. We need a comprehensive plan now to reduce the debt over the long term. But budget cuts should start gradually so they don't interfere with the ongoing economic recovery. Growth is essential to restoring fiscal strength and balance.

Cut and invest to promote economic growth and keep America competitive. We should cut red tape and unproductive government spending that hinders job creation and growth. At the same time, we must invest in education, infrastructure, and high-value research and development to help our economy grow, keep us globally competitive, and make it easier for businesses to create jobs.

Protect the truly disadvantaged. We must ensure that our nation has a robust, affordable, fair, and sustainable safety net. Benefits should be focused on those who need them the most.

Cut spending we cannot afford – no exceptions. We must end redundant, wasteful, and ineffective federal spending, wherever we find it. We should cut <u>all</u> excess spending – including defense, domestic programs, entitlement spending, and spending in the tax code.

Demand productivity and effectiveness from Washington. We must use fiscal restraint to promote reforms and efficiencies that force government to produce better results and save money. We should insist on consistent productivity growth in our government.

Reform and simplify the tax code. The tax code is rife with inefficiencies, loopholes, incentives, tax earmarks, and baffling complexity. We need to lower tax rates, broaden the base, simplify the tax code, and bring down the deficit. We need to reform the corporate tax system to make America the best place to start and grow a business and create jobs.

Don't make promises we can't keep. Our country has tough choices to make. We need to be willing to tell Americans the truth: We cannot afford to continue spending more than we take in, and we cannot continue to make promises we know full well we cannot keep.

The problem is real, and the solution will be painful. We must stabilize and then reduce the national debt, or we could spend $1 trillion a year in interest alone by 2020. There is no easy way out of our debt problem, so everything must be on the table. A sensible, realistic plan requires shared sacrifice – and Washington must lead the way and tighten its belt.

Keep America sound over the long run. We need to implement policies today to ensure that future generations have retirement security, affordable health care, and financial freedom. To do that, we must make Social Security solvent and sound, reduce the long-term growth of health care spending, and tackle the nation's overwhelming debt burden.

Overview

We propose a six-part plan to put our nation back on a path to fiscal health, promote economic growth, and protect the most vulnerable among us. Taken as a whole, the plan will:

- Achieve nearly $4 trillion in deficit reduction through 2020, more than any effort in the nation's history.

- Reduce the deficit to 2.3% of GDP by 2015 (2.4% excluding Social Security reform), exceeding President's goal of primary balance (about 3% of GDP).[2]

- Sharply reduce tax rates, abolish the AMT, and cut backdoor spending in the tax code.

- Cap revenue at 21% of GDP and get spending below 22% and eventually to 21%.

- Ensure lasting Social Security solvency, prevent the projected 22% cuts to come in 2037, reduce elderly poverty, and distribute the burden fairly.

- Stabilize debt by 2014 and reduce debt to 60% of GDP by 2023 and 40% by 2035.

Figure 2: Annual Deficits Under Commission Proposal (as percent of GDP)

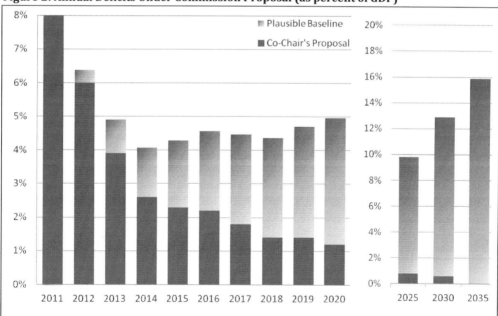

Note: Plausible baseline resembles CBO's Alternative Fiscal Scenario, assuming the continuation of the 2001/2003 tax cuts protected by Statutory PAYGO, estate tax and AMT policies at 2009 levels, and a Medicare physicians' pay freeze. The baseline also assumes discretionary spending as requested in the President's Budget and a gradual phase down of the conflicts in Iraq and Afghanistan.

---

[2] Note that increases in this deficit level as compared to the Co-Chairs' November 10, 2010, draft do not reflect major policy changes, but rather baseline changes to more honestly (and conservatively) account for the costs of the conflicts in Iraq and Afghanistan

The plan has six major components:

1) **Discretionary Spending Cuts:** Enact tough discretionary spending caps to force budget discipline in Congress. Include enforcement mechanisms to give the limits real teeth. Make significant cuts in both security and non-security spending by cutting low-priority programs and streamlining government operations. Offer over $50 billion in immediate cuts to lead by example, and provide $200 billion in illustrative 2015 savings.

2) **Comprehensive Tax Reform:** Sharply reduce rates, broaden the base, simplify the tax code, and reduce the deficit by reducing the many "tax expenditures"—another name for spending through the tax code. Reform corporate taxes to make America more competitive, and cap revenue to avoid excessive taxation.

3) **Health Care Cost Containment:** Replace the phantom savings from scheduled Medicare reimbursement cuts that will never materialize and from a new long-term care program that is unsustainable with real, common-sense reforms to physician payments, cost-sharing, malpractice law, prescription drug costs, government-subsidized medical education, and other sources. Institute additional long-term measures to bring down spending growth.

Figure 3: Deficit Reduction Under Commission Proposal (in billions)

	2012	2013	2014	2015	2016	2017	2018	2019	2020	2012-2015	2012-2020
Discretionary Spending	*$49*	*$102*	*$141*	*$172*	*$194*	*$215*	*$236*	*$261*	*$291*	*$464*	*$1,661*
Mandatory Spending	*$1*	*$32*	*$47*	*$54*	*$64*	*$70*	*$88*	*$97*	*$104*	*$134*	*$556*
Spending in the Tax Code / Tax Reform	*$0*	*$20*	*$40*	*$80*	*$90*	*$105*	*$120*	*$150*	*$180*	*$140*	*$785*
Other Revenue	*$1*	*$5*	*$11*	*$18*	*$27*	*$32*	*$36*	*$39*	*$43*	*$34*	*$210*
Net Interest Savings	*$1*	*$5*	*$16*	*$33*	*$58*	*$87*	*$119*	*$155*	*$199*	*$56*	*$673*
Total Deficit Reduction*	**$52**	**$164**	**$255**	**$357**	**$433**	**$509**	**$599**	**$702**	**$817**	**$828**	**$3,885**
Projected Deficit Under Plan (*excluding* Social Security reform)	-$943	-$655	-$469	**-$440**	-$456	-$404	-$332	-$343	-$333		
	-6.0%	-3.9%	-2.7%	**-2.4%**	-2.4%	-2.0%	-1.6%	-1.6%	-1.5%		
Projected Deficit Under Plan (*including* Social Security reform)	-$949	-$646	-$455	**-$421**	-$432	-$372	-$294	-$298	-$279		
	-6.0%	-3.9%	-2.6%	**-2.3%**	-2.2%	-1.8%	-1.4%	-1.3%	-1.2%		

*Note: Excludes Social Security

4) **Mandatory Savings:** Cut agriculture subsidies and modernize military and civil service retirement systems, while reforming student loan programs and putting the Pension Benefit Guarantee Corporation on a sustainable path.

5) **Social Security Reforms to Ensure Long-Term Solvency and Reduce Poverty:** Ensure sustainable solvency for the next 75 years while reducing poverty among seniors. Reform Social Security for its own sake, and not for deficit reduction.

6) **Process Changes:** Reform the budget process to ensure the debt remains on a stable path, spending stays under control, inflation is measured accurately, and taxpayer dollars go where they belong.

Figure 4: Federal Outlays, Revenue, Deficit, and Debt Under Commission Proposal (as percent of GDP)

	Outlays	Revenue	Deficit	Debt
2010	23.8%	14.9%	-8.9%	62%
2015	21.6%	19.3%	-2.3%	70%
2020	21.8%	20.6%	-1.2%	65%
2025	21.8%	21.0%	-0.8%	57%
2030	21.6%	21.0%	-0.6%	49%
2035	21.0%	21.0%	0.0%	40%

The Plan

I. Discretionary Spending Cuts

Over the past decade, base discretionary spending (excluding war costs) has grown by 34 percent in inflation-adjusted dollars (64 percent in nominal dollars), and the President's Fiscal Year 2011budget projects it to grow by an additional 6 percent to $1.26 trillion in 2015. In order to bring down the deficit, Washington will have to rein in discretionary spending. Every aspect of the discretionary budget must be scrutinized, no agency can be off limits, and no program that spends too much or achieves too little can be spared. The federal government can and must adapt to the 21st century by transforming itself into a leaner and more efficient operation. Like its citizens, government must also be willing to do more with less and live within its means.

As the Chairman of the Joint Chiefs of Staff, Admiral Mike Mullen, has noted, the most significant threat to our national security is our debt. The ability of the United States to keep our country secure over time depends on restoring fiscal restraint today. Any serious attempt to reduce the deficit will require deliberate, planned reductions in both domestic and defense spending. The government will not be able to protect those in need or invest to achieve our nation's long-term potential growth if Washington squanders taxpayer dollars on duplicative programs with no measurable results.

In the 1990s, discretionary spending caps played a large role in bringing the budget into balance. By establishing formidable boundaries to guide spending in future years, Congress and the Administration will be forced to eliminate waste and excess in bloated agency budgets, better target funding toward programs that demonstrate real results, and reduce duplication throughout the federal bureaucracy.

The spending path recommended by the Commission is more than simply numbers on a page. It is a vision for our future reflecting the values and priorities of the American people. We must continue to invest in our future, but must not undermine those investments by leaving generations yet to come with a debt they cannot repay. The Commission's spending limits will necessitate a more efficient government that invests wisely, spends Americans' precious tax dollars well, and is transparent and accountable for every dime.

RECOMMENDATION 1.1: CAP DISCRETIONARY SPENDING THROUGH 2020. Hold spending in 2012 equal to or lower than spending in 2011, and return spending to pre-crisis 2008 levels in real terms in 2013. Limit future spending growth to half the projected inflation rate through 2020.

Under the Commission proposal, discretionary spending would be frozen at 2011 levels* in 2012, and brought down to inflation-adjusted pre-crisis levels in 2013. This path would require serious belt-tightening to begin in 2012, followed by substantial nominal cuts in 2013. Underlying this path is an expectation that the government will need to decide what it can no longer afford to do. Over the next 18 months, agencies will need to undertake a thorough review of their budgets, working with the Office of Management and Budget (OMB) to identify ineffective and redundant efforts, and distinguishing between core services and programs that have simply continued through inertia. Congress will also need to critically review all funded programs and make tough decisions to set priorities and reform or eliminate a number of them. Although this process is especially important in the short-term, before of 2013, it should be considered an essential part of an ongoing course of action to assess and reassess budget priorities. The Government Accountability Office (GAO) should be tasked to assist in this effort by identifying redundancies and reviewing performance, where possible.

Beyond 2013, discretionary spending caps will demand continued efficiencies from the government by holding spending growth to about half the rate of inflation. This approach will help bring spending under control immediately, but do so in a way that takes into account the fragile recovery in the near term and allows Congress and the President time to carefully evaluate budget priorities going forward. Moreover, these caps would serve as a ceiling rather than a floor – so members of Congress would be free to cut spending below the caps in the appropriations process.

The path would be as follows:

Figure 5: Discretionary Path Under Commission Proposal

Commission Proposal	2012	2013	2014	2015	2016	2017	2018	2019	2020	2012-2015	2012-2020
Total	1,098*	1,043	1,050	**1,061**	1,072	1,084	1,095	1,106	1,117	4,251	9,724
Security	688*	654	658	**665**	672	679	686	693	700	2,664	6,095
Non-security	410*	389	393	**396**	400	405	409	413	417	1,587	3,630
President's Request	1,180	1,196	1,229	**1,266**	1,293	1,324	1,359	1,397	1,442	4,872	11,686
CBO baseline	1,143	1,164	1,191	**1,222**	1,257	1,290	1,323	1,357	1,390	4,720	11,337
Dollar amount below President	84*	153	179	**205**	221	240	264	291	325	622	1,963
Percentage below President's request	7.1%	12.8%	14.6%	**16.2%**	17.1%	18.1%	19.4%	20.8%	22.5%	12.8%	16.8%
Outlay savings	60	113	152	**183**	205	226	247	272	302	508	1,760

*Note: Levels will be set by the current Congress rather than the statutory caps, and that the 2012 levels will be at or below the final 2011 levels. $1098 represents a 12-month Continuing Resolution as a default, but the actual number could differ significantly.

RECOMMENDATION 1.2: CUT BOTH SECURITY AND NON-SECURITY SPENDING. Establish firewall between the two categories through 2015, and require equal percentage cuts from both sides.

One of the Commission's guiding principles is that everything must be on the table. In order to achieve real spending discipline, Congress and the President must be willing to cut excess spending wherever they find it.

Past budget agreements in 1990, 1993, and 1997 established firewalls between defense and non-defense expenditures, requiring savings from both categories to keep spending levels below the caps. Some past firewalls have also separated international affairs and other categories. With new homeland security expenditures and increased spending on veterans and international affairs, though, a firewall between security and non-security spending is appropriate.

The security category would include all defense spending, although for purposes of the caps we address war spending separately. It would also include spending on nuclear weapons, homeland security, veterans, and international affairs. All security spending, which constitutes about two-thirds of the discretionary budget, has one overriding goal: to keep the nation safe. The remaining third of the discretionary budget is dedicated to non-security programs – the large array of domestic activities, including education, housing, law enforcement, research, public health, culture, poverty reduction, and other programs.

The spending caps will remain in place through 2020, but consistent with past agreements, the firewalls will lapse after 2015 in case adjustments in the balance between categories become necessary.

RECOMMENDATION 1.3: ENFORCE CAPS THROUGH TWO MECHANISMS -- POINT OF ORDER AND ABATEMENT. Require a separate non-amendable vote in House and 60-vote point of order in Senate to spend above the caps. If caps are exceeded, impose across-the-board abatement by the amount appropriations exceed the caps.

Tough discretionary spending caps must be accompanied by tough enforcement. The Commission recommends establishing a belt-and-suspenders approach that enforces discretionary caps through both a front-end point of order (to block passage of a bill that exceeds the caps) and a back-end, across-the-board abatement (to cut spending by an amount sufficient to bring it back in line with the caps if the point of order is waived). The Senate would not be able to proceed to a vote on final passage of an appropriations bill as amended by the Senate until there is a final score of the bill from the Budget Committee. If the score shows that the bill would exceed its allocation or result in the discretionary spending limit being exceeded, it would be in order to consider a motion to re commit the bill with instructions to reduce spending in the bill.

At the end of the session, CBO must certify that discretionary spending approved by Congress was within the caps. If the caps are not met, OMB will be required to implement an across-the-board abatement.

Any appropriations bill that would cause the caps to be breached – as well as any legislation to suspend an abatement – would be subject to a point of order blocking passage of the bill. The point of order could be waived only with a separate non-amendable vote in the House and a separate vote in the Senate requiring 60 votes in favor. A budget resolution recommending discretionary spending in excess of the caps in any year would lose its privileged status, effectively then requiring 60 votes in the Senate.

RECOMMENDATION 1.4: REQUIRE THE PRESIDENT TO PROPOSE ANNUAL LIMITS FOR WAR SPENDING. Create a separate category for Overseas Contingency Operations (OCO).

Discretionary spending constraints must not ignore spending for the conflicts in Iraq and Afghanistan and other future conflicts. At the same time, budget rules should not determine war policy. In order to balance these competing goals, the Commission chose as a starting point the more gradual of CBO's troop drawdown scenario, while providing the President and Congress with an opportunity to adjust the path to more accurately track with actual projections of OCO spending needs.

Spending for OCO would not count against the general security spending cap, but would constitute a separate category subject to a dollar limit of its own. The Commission proposes establishing limits on OCO spending based on CBO's projection for a reduction of troop levels to 60,000 by 2015. In his FY 2012 budget, the President may propose adjustments to the limits on OCO spending to reflect the administration's projections for the costs of current war policy. Any spending above the OCO limit must be either offset or subject to a 60-vote point of order (and all other requirements established for regular emergency spending).

OCO funds would be limited to spending that meets the OMB criteria for OCO designation. Under these criteria funding for OCO could only be used in geographic areas in which combat or direct combat support operations occur, and would generally be limited to: 1) Operations and maintenance for the transport of personnel, equipment, and supplies to, from and within the theater of operations; deployment-specific training and preparation for units and personnel to assume their directed mission; and the incremental costs above the funding programmed in the base budget to build and maintain temporary facilities; provide food, fuel, supplies, contracted services and other support; and cover the operational costs of coalition partners supporting US military missions; 2) Military personnel spending for incremental special pays and allowances for Service members and civilians deployed to a combat zone; and incremental pay, special pays and allowances for Reserve Component personnel mobilized to support war missions; 3) Procurement costs to replace losses that have occurred, but only for items not already programmed for replacement in the Future Years Defense Plan; 4) Military construction spending for facilities and infrastructure in the theater of operations in direct support of combat operations; and 5) Research and development projects required for combat operations in these specific theaters that can be delivered in 12 months.

RECOMMENDATION 1.5: ESTABLISH A DISASTER FUND TO BUDGET HONESTLY FOR CATASTROPHES.

Restoring fiscal discipline requires honest budgeting. Any given disaster may itself be unpredictable, but the need to pay for some level of disaster relief is not. Yet federal budgets rarely set aside adequate resources in anticipation of such disasters, and instead rely on emergency supplemental funding requests. The Commission plan explicitly sets aside funds for disaster relief and establishes stricter parameters for the use of these funds.

The disaster fund budget authority (BA) will be limited to the rolling average of disaster spending in the most recent 10 years, excluding the highest and lowest year. Any unused budget authority will be rolled forward to increase the disaster fund BA available in the following year. Any spending above the disaster fund limit must be offset with reductions in spending or subject to a 60-vote point of order (and all other requirements established for regular emergency spending).

The Commission recommends codifying a strict definition of what qualifies as a disaster, and requiring Congress and the President to separately designate spending as an emergency and as necessary for the purposes of disaster response.

To keep Congress accountable and encourage transparency, the Commission also recommends the establishment of a searchable online database of all disaster spending, similar to that found on the Recovery.gov website, to be maintained by the Government Accountability Office and operational by January 1, 2012.

RECOMMENDATION 1.6: STOP THE ABUSE OF EMERGENCY SPENDING.

In limited situations, some emergency costs may be necessary. However, such spending must be subject to far greater accountability and transparency that it is today. Too often, Congress uses the emergency designation as a loophole to get around fiscal restraints. The Commission proposes several steps to make sure the emergency designation is used only for true emergencies.

Congress should codify a strict, clear legal definition of emergency, such as the one used by the Office of Management and Budget. Both houses should only use the emergency designation to address urgent needs for costs that cannot be reasonably offset. Further, Congress should designate each emergency provision individually and discontinue the practice of using global designations. In the Senate, an emergency designation would be in order only if (1) the proposed cost is certified as an emergency by the Senate Budget Committee, pursuant to this definition; and (2) a point of order against the designation, if raised on the Senate floor, is waived by at least a three-fifths majority. The House would require designation either from the Budget Committee or through a separate, non-amendable vote.

Costs not designated as emergency would be subject to discretionary spending caps, statutory PAYGO, and any other enforceable budgetary limits agreed by Congress, such as the Commission's proposed debt stabilization process.

RECOMMENDATION 1.7: FULLY FUND THE TRANSPORTATION TRUST FUND INSTEAD OF RELYING ON DEFICIT SPENDING. Dedicate a 15-cent per gallon increase in the gas tax to transportation funding, and limit spending if necessary to match the revenues the trust fund collects each year.

Under current law, the Transportation Trust Fund has hybrid budget treatment in which contract authority is mandatory, while outlays are discretionary. This hybrid treatment results in less accountability and discipline for transportation spending and allows for budget gimmicks to circumvent budget limits to increase spending. The Commission plan reclassifies spending from the Transportation Trust Fund to make both contract authority and outlays mandatory, and then limits spending to actual revenues collected by the trust fund in the prior year once the gas tax is fully phased in. Shortfalls up until that point would be financed by the general fund.

The Commission recommends gradually increasing the per gallon gas tax by 15 cents between 2013 and 2015. Congress must limit spending from trust funds to the level of dedicated revenues from the previous year. Before asking taxpayers to pay more for roads, rail, bridges, and infrastructure, we must ensure existing funds are not wasted. The Commission recommends significant reforms to control federal highway spending. Congress should limit trust fund spending to the most pressing infrastructure needs rather than forcing states to fund low-priority projects. It should also end the practice of highway authorization earmarks such as the infamous Bridge to Nowhere.

RECOMMENDATION 1.8: UNLEASH AGENCIES TO BEGIN IDENTIFYING SAVINGS.

Every federal agency will need to do its part to live within tough spending caps. The Commission recommends that as part of their annual budget submissions and Congressional Budget Justifications, all agency heads should be required to identify a share of their budget recommended for cancellation and to identify ways to shift from inefficient, unproductive spending to productive, results-based investment. As a tool to improve productivity, agencies should be given a two-year window to conduct employee buyouts, and expanded latitude for personnel realignment. Congress should also consider a "BRAC commission" for terminating major weapons systems, appointed and headed by the Secretary of Defense, for trimming redundant or ineffective weapons from the Defense Department's inventory.

RECOMMENDATION 1.9: ESTABLISH CUT-AND-INVEST COMMITTEE TO CUT LOW-PRIORITY SPENDING, INCREASE HIGH-PRIORITY INVESTMENT, AND CONSOLIDATE DUPLICATIVE FEDERAL PROGRAMS.

The Commission recommends creating a new, bipartisan Cut-and-Invest Committee to be charged each year with identifying 2 percent of the discretionary budget that should be cut and identifying how to redirect half of that savings, or 1 percent, into high-value investment. Over the next decade, the Cut-and-Invest Committee will be expected to recommend more than $200 billion in discretionary cuts, freeing up $100 billion for high-priority investments America will need to remain competitive, such as increasing college graduation rates, leveraging private capital through an infrastructure bank, and expanding high-value research and development in energy and other critical areas.

The significant growth in domestic spending over the last decade has brought an alarming proliferation of federal programs – many of which duplicate pre-existing federal efforts and each other. Instead of eliminating outdated or ineffective initiatives, Congress often simply creates more programs to address the same concerns. The result is a patchwork of thousands of duplicative programs, nearly impossible to track and even harder to evaluate for effective outcomes. Duplication results in unnecessary deficit spending and crowds out important investments.

For example, the government funds more than 44 job training programs across nine different federal agencies, at least 20 programs at 12 agencies dedicated to the study of invasive species, and 105 programs meant to encourage participation in science, technology, education, and math. Many of these programs cannot demonstrate to Congress or taxpayers they are actually accomplishing their intended purpose. Programs without demonstrable results costs taxpayers billions of dollars and fail those the programs are intended to serve. The Government Accountability Office (GAO) will soon release its first annual duplication review of overlapping federal programs, agencies, and initiatives. The Commission recommends that in 2011, congressional authorizing committees report out legislation to consolidate and eliminate duplicative programs within their jurisdiction, and that Congress rescind savings from reduced overhead and program elimination.

RECOMMENDATION 1.10: ADOPT IMMEDIATE REFORMS TO REDUCE SPENDING AND MAKE THE FEDERAL GOVERNMENT MORE EFFICIENT.

In addition to these proposals, the Commission advises that through executive action, congressional rule, and legislation, a number of steps be taken immediately to show Washington can lead by example. The collected recommendations that follow wouldreduce spending on both the security and non-security sides of the discretionary budget. Together, they will save more than $50 billion in 2015 alone:

1.10.1 Reduce Congressional and White House budgets by 15 percent. Although the nation's economy continues to struggle, there's no recession in Washington. Like most areas of government, the budgets for Congress and the Executive Office of the President have grown significantly in recent years. For example, spending on the legislative branch rose close to 50 percent from FY 2000 through FY 2010. Last year Congress gave itself a nearly four percent budget increase. In order to tackle our impending fiscal crisis, everyone must sacrifice – especially Washington. The Commission's proposal would reduce the budgets for Congress and the White House by 15 percent. This proposal will save $800 million in 2015.

1.10.2 Impose a three-year freeze on Member pay. Unlike most Americans, members of Congress benefit from an automatic salary increase every single year – deserved or not. Before Congress can ask the American people to sacrifice, it should lead by example. The Commission recommends an immediate three-year salary freeze for all members of Congress.

1.10.3 Impose a three-year pay freeze on federal workers and Defense Department civilians. Out of duty and patriotism, hardworking federal employees provide a great service to this country. But in a time of budget shortfalls, all levels of government must trim back. In the recent recession, millions of private sector and state and municipal employees had their wages frozen or cut back, and millions more lost their jobs altogether. In contrast, federal workers' wages increase annually due to automatic formulas in law, providing them with cost-of-living-adjustments totaling more than five percent in the last two years. This proposal would institute a three-year government-wide freeze on federal pay at every government agency, including the Department of Defense civilian workforce. This proposal will save $20.4 billion in 2015.

1.10.4 Reduce the size of the federal workforce through attrition. The federal government currently employs about two million people, and extends federal staffing through thousands more contractors. Washington needs to learn to do more with less, using fewer resources to accomplish existing goals without risking a decline in essential government services. Over time, the Commission recommends cutting the government workforce – including civilian defense – by 10 percent, or by 200,000. As part of the transition to a smaller, more efficient workforce, this would mean hiring only two new workers for every three who leave service. This proposal will save $13.2 billion in 2015.

1.10.5 Reduce federal travel, printing, and vehicle budgets. Despite advances in technology, federal travel costs have ballooned in recent years, growing 56 percent between 2001 and 2006 alone. Government fleets, meanwhile, have grown by 20,000 over the last four years. Printing costs are still higher than necessary despite technological advancement. We propose prohibiting each agency from spending more than 80 percent of its FY 2010 travel budget and requiring them to do more through teleconferencing and telecommuting. We also recommend a 20 percent reduction in the nearly $4 billion annual federal vehicle budget, excluding the Department of Defense and the Postal Service. Additionally, we recommend allowing certain documents to be released in electronic-only form, and capping total government printing expenditures. This proposal will save $1.1 billion in 2015.

1.10.6 Sell excess federal real property. The federal government is the largest real property owner in the country, with an inventory of more than 1.2 million buildings, structures, and land parcels. Holding this unneeded property carries maintenance costs and forgoes the opportunity to sell potentially valuable property. We propose directing the GSA to loosen agency restrictions associated with selling unused buildings and land. This proposal will save at least $100 million in 2015.

1.10.7 Eliminate all congressional earmarks. In FY 2010, Congress approved more than 9,000 earmarks costing taxpayers close to $16 billion. Earmarks are not competitively bid and are not subject to accountability metrics, making it difficult to measure effectiveness or conduct cost-benefit analysis. Many of these earmarks are doled out by members of Congress for parochial concerns in their districts and to special interest groups. Examples of parochial earmark spending include $1.9 million for a Pleasure Beach Water Taxi Service in Connecticut, $900,000 for a program encouraging Oklahoma students to role-play how to make tough choices as members of Congress, and $238,000 for ancient-style sailing canoes in Hawaii, among countless others. The Commission recommends the elimination of all congressional appropriations and authorizing earmarks as well as limited tax and tariff benefits. This proposal will save at least $16 billion in 2015.

RECOMMENDATION 1.11: FIND ADDITIONAL CUTS IN SECURITY AND NON-SECURITY SPENDING.

To meet the discretionary spending caps we recommend above, Congress will have to make tough choices. The list of illustrative savings options accompanying this report includes $200 billion in potential savings in security and non-security discretionary spending. This list includes more than enough specific savings options to meet our proposed caps. Although not every option is supported by every Commissioner, this list is included to illustrate a realistic, feasible path Congress could take to rein in discretionary spending.

II. Tax Reform

America's tax code is broken and must be reformed. In the quarter century since the last comprehensive tax reform, Washington has riddled the system with countless tax expenditures, which are simply spending by another name. These tax earmarks – amounting to $1.1 trillion a year of spending in the tax code – not only increase the deficit, but cause tax rates to be too high. Instead of promoting economic growth and competitiveness, our current code drives up health care costs and provides special treatment to special interests. The code presents individuals and businesses with perverse economic incentives instead of a level playing field.

The current individual income tax system is hopelessly confusing and complicated. Many taxpayers are required to make multiple computations to see if they qualify for a number of benefits and penalties, and many dole out large sums of money to tax preparers. Meanwhile, other taxpayers underreport their income and taxes, hoping to avoid the audit lottery. In short, the Commission has concluded what most taxpayers already know – the current income tax is fundamentally unfair, far too complex, and long overdue for sweeping reform.

The corporate income tax, meanwhile, hurts America's ability to compete. On the one hand, statutory rates in the U.S. are significantly higher than the average for industrialized countries (even as revenue collection is low), and our method of taxing foreign income is outside the norm. The U.S. is one of the only industrialized countries with a hybrid system of taxing active foreign-source income. The current system puts U.S. corporations at a competitive disadvantage against their foreign competitors. A territorial tax system should be adopted to help put the U.S. system in line with other countries, leveling the playing field.

Tax reform should lower tax rates, reduce the deficit, simplify the tax code, reduce the tax gap, and make America the best place to start a business and create jobs. Rather than tinker around the edges of the existing tax code, the Commission proposes fundamental and comprehensive tax reform that achieves these basic goals:

Lower rates, broaden the base, and cut spending in the tax code. The current tax code is riddled with $1.1 trillion of tax expenditures: backdoor spending hidden in the tax code. Tax reform must reduce the size and number of these tax expenditures and lower marginal tax rates for individuals and corporations – thereby simplifying the code, improving fairness, reducing the tax gap, and spurring economic growth. Simplifying the code will dramatically reduce the cost and burden of tax preparation and compliance for individuals and corporations.

Reduce the deficit. To escape our nation's crushing debt and deficit problem, we must have shared sacrifice – and that means a portion of the savings from cutting tax expenditures must be dedicated to deficit reduction. At the same time, revenue cannot constantly increase as a share of the economy. Deficit reduction from tax reform will be companied by deficit reduction from spending cuts—which will come first. Under our plan, revenue reaches 21 percent of GDP by 2022 and is then capped at that level.

Maintain or increase progressivity of the tax code. Though reducing the deficit will require shared sacrifice, those of us who are best off will need to contribute the most. Tax reform must continue to protect those who are most vulnerable, and eliminate tax loopholes favoring those who need help least.

Make America the best place to start a business and create jobs. The current tax code saps the competitiveness of U.S. companies. Tax reform should make the United States the best place for starting and building businesses. Additionally, the tax code should help U.S.-based multinationals compete abroad in active foreign operations and in acquiring foreign businesses.

RECOMMENDATION 2.1: ENACT FUNDAMENTAL TAX REFORM BY 2012 TO LOWER RATES, REDUCE DEFICITS, AND SIMPLIFY THE CODE. Eliminate all income tax expenditures, dedicate a portion of the additional revenue to deficit reduction, and use the remaining revenue to lower rates and add back necessary expenditures and credits.

Fundamental tax reform will require significant revisions to the current tax code and will need to take into account the transition to new and modified provisions. These tasks are not insignificant and the Commission recognizes that for Congress and the President to consider and implement these sweeping changes, a comprehensive process will be needed. To this end, the Commission recommends requiring the House Committee on Ways and Means and the Senate Committee on Finance, in cooperation with the Department of the Treasury, to report out comprehensive tax reform legislation through a fast track process by 2012.

The Commission proposes tax reform that relies on "zero-base budgeting" by eliminating all income tax expenditures (but maintaining the current payroll tax base, which should be modified only in the context of Social Security reform), and then using the revenue to lower rates and reduce deficits. The revenue from eliminating tax expenditures should be dedicated to three clear purposes: 1) substantially lowering marginal tax rates; 2) reducing the reduction; and 3) supporting a small number of simpler, more targeted provisions that promote work, home ownership, health care, charity, and savings. As a matter of principle, tax reform must increase or maintain progressivity.

A "zero plan" could reduce income tax rates to as low as 8%, 14%, and 23%. Even after adding back a number of larger tax expenditures, rates would still remain significantly lower than under current law.

Figure 6: Tax Rates Under Various Scenarios

	Bottom Rate		Middle Rate		Top Rate		Corporate Rate
Current Rates for 2010	10%	15%	25%	28%	33%	35%	35%
Scheduled Rates for 2011	15%		28%	31%	36%	39.6%	35%
Eliminate all Tax Expenditures*	8%		14%		23%		26%
Keep Child Tax Credit + EITC*	9%		15%		24%		26%
Enact Illustrative Tax Plan (Below)*	12%		22%		28%		28%

*Dedicates $80 billion to deficit reduction in 2015 and taxes capital gains and dividends as ordinary income.

29

In designing tax reform, Congress must abide by the following parameters in order to receive a fast-tracked status:

2.1.1 Cut rates across the board, and reduce the top rate to between 23 and 29 percent. Real tax reform must dedicate a portion of the savings from cutting tax expenditures to lowering individual rates. The top rate must not exceed 29%.

2.1.2 Dedicate $80 billion to deficit reduction in 2015 and $180 billion in 2020. In additional to reducing rates, reform must be projected to raise $80 billion of additional revenue (relative to the alternative fiscal scenario) in 2015 and $180 billion in 2020. To the extent that the dynamic effects of tax reform result in additional revenue beyond these targets, excess funds must go to rate reductions and deficit reduction, not to new spending.

2.1.3 Simplify key provisions to promote work, homes, health, charity, and savings while increasing or maintaining progressivity. Congress and the President must decide which tax expenditures to include in the tax code in smaller and more targeted form than under current law, recognizing that any add-backs will raise rates. The new tax code must include provisions (in some cases permanent, in others temporary) for the following:

- Support for low-income workers and families (e.g., the child credit and EITC);
- Mortgage interest only for principal residences;
- Employer-provided health insurance;
- Charitable giving;
- Retirement savings and pensions.

Additional tax expenditures could be added to the provisions above, but <u>must</u> be paid for with higher rates. Furthermore, the revised code must increase or maintain progressivity, across the income spectrum, relative to the alternative fiscal scenario. In enacting tax reform, Congress and the President should design appropriate transition rules that minimize economic distortions, achieve the necessary revenue targets, and allow taxpayers to adapt to the changes.

Though the precise details and exact transition rules should be worked out in a variety of ways by the relevant congressional committees and the Treasury Department, the Commission has designed an illustrative set of reforms that would accomplish the necessary parameters for tax reform.

The plan below is an illustrative attempt to reflect the priorities of Commission members, but Congress could choose different options. We developed this illustrative plan to demonstrate that it is possible both to reduce rates dramatically and to achieve significant deficit reduction if tax expenditures are eliminated or scaled back and better targeted.

Figure 7: Illustrative Individual Tax Reform Plan

	Current Law	Illustrative Proposal (Fully Phased In)
Tax rates for Individuals	In **2010**, six brackets: 10%|15%|25%| 28%|33%|35%. In **2011**, five brackets: 15%|28%|31%|36%|39.6%	Three brackets: 12%|22%|28%
Alternative Minimum Tax	Scheduled to hit middle-income individuals but "patched" annually	Permanently repealed
PEP and Pease[3]	Repealed for **2010**, resumes in **2011**	Permanently repealed
EITC and Child Tax Credit	Partially refundable child tax credit of $1000 per child. Refundable EITC of between $457 and $5,666	Maintain current law or an equivalent alternative
Standard Deduction and Exemptions	Standard deduction of $5,700 ($11,400 for couple) for non-itemizers; personal and dependent exemptions of $3,650	Maintain current law; itemized deductions eliminated, so all individuals take standard deductions
Capital Gains and Dividends	In **2010**, top rate of 15% for capital gains and dividends. In **2011**, top rate of 20% for capital gains, and dividends taxed as ordinary income[4]	All capital gains and dividends taxed at ordinary income rates[5]
Mortgage Interest	Deductible for itemizers; Mortgage capped at $1 million for principal and second residences, plus an additional $100,000 for home equity	12% non-refundable tax credit available to all taxpayers; Mortgage capped at $500,000; No credit for interest from second residence and equity
Employer Provided Health Care Insurance	Excluded from income. 40% excise tax on high cost plans (generally $27,500 for families) begins in 2018; threshold indexed to inflation	Exclusion capped at 75th percentile of premium levels in 2014, with cap frozen in nominal terms through 2018 and phased out by 2038; Excise tax reduced to 12%
Charitable Giving	Deductible for itemizers	12% non-refundable tax credit available to all taxpayers; available above 2% of Adjusted Gross Income (AGI) floor
State and Municipal Bonds	Interest exempt from income	Interest taxable as income for newly-issued bonds
Retirement	Multiple retirement account options with different contribution limits; saver's credit of up to $1,000	Consolidate retirement accounts; cap tax-preferred contributions to lower of $20,000 or 20% of income, expand saver's credit
Other Tax Expenditures	Over 150 additional tax expenditures	Nearly all other income tax expenditures are eliminated[6]

---

3 PEP is the Personal Exemption Phase-out; Pease is the phase-out of itemized deductions. PEP and Pease have phase-outs at different levels and are viewed as stealth taxes.

4 Collectibles (e.g., coin, art, antiques) are taxed at 28% and unrecaptured gain on real estate is taxed at 25%.

5 An alternative could be to exclude a portion of capital gains and dividends from income (e.g. 20%), reducing the effective top rate on investment income. To offset this while maintaining progressivity in the code, the top rate on ordinary income would need to be increased.

6 Under this plan, a few tax expenditures remain, for instance no changes are made to the tax treatment of employer pensions and tax provisions under PPACA largely remain in place. Note that the *payroll tax* base would remain the same as under current law, though there will be secondary revenue effects on the payroll tax side.

Below is a preliminary distributional analysis of a plan similar to the Illustrative Individual Tax Plan put together by the Tax Policy Center. This estimate assumes rates of 12.7%, 21%, and 28% (instead of 12% 22%, and 28%). They also include the effects of the gas tax and other tax provisions elsewhere in our proposal. Rates of 12%, 22%, and 28%, as described in the illustrative plan, would result in a slightly more progressive outcome.

Figure 8: Illustrative Distributional Analysis

Cash Income Percentile	Percent Change in After-Tax Income	Share of Total Federal Tax Change	Average Federal Tax Change	
			Dollars	Percent
Bottom Quintile	-0.2	0.4	24	4.1
2nd Quintile	-1.6	5.9	464	13.5
Middle Quintile	-1.5	8.4	722	7.2
4th Quintile	-1.5	11.5	1,193	5.8
Top Quintile	-3.7	73.5	8,686	10.4
All	-2.6	100.0	1,746	9.3
Addendum				
80-90	-2.0	10.0	2,354	6.5
90-95	-1.9	6.7	3,203	6.0
95-99	-1.7	8.6	5,114	5.0
Top 1 Percent	-7.8	48.2	112,533	18.0
Top 0.1 Percent	-11.8	32.1	735,172	24.0

Source: Urban-Brookings Tax Policy Center Microsimulation Model (version 0509-4).

RECOMMENDATION 2.2: ENACT CORPORATE REFORM TO LOWER RATES, CLOSE LOOPHOLES, AND MOVE TO A TERRITORIAL SYSTEM.

The U.S. corporate tax is a patchwork of overly complex and inefficient provisions that creates perverse incentives for investment. Corporations engage in self-help to decrease their tax liability and improve their bottom line. Moreover, corporations are able to minimize tax through various tax expenditures inserted into the tax code as a result of successful lobbying.

Without reform, it is likely that U.S. competitiveness will continue to suffer. The results of inaction are undesirable: the loss of American jobs, the movement of business operations overseas, reduced investment by foreign businesses in the U.S., reduced innovation and creation of intellectual property in the U.S., the sale of U.S. companies to foreign multinationals, and a general erosion of the corporate tax base.

Reform of the corporate tax structure should include the following:

2.2.1 Establish single corporate tax rate between 23 percent and 29 percent. Corporate tax reform should replace the multiple brackets (the top being 35 percent), with a single bracket as low as 23 percent and no higher than 29 percent.

2.2.2 Eliminate all tax expenditures for businesses. Corporate tax reform should eliminate special subsidies for different industries. By eliminating business tax expenditures – currently more than 75 – the corporate tax rate can be significantly reduced while contributing to deficit reduction. A lower overall tax rate will improve American business competitiveness. Abolishing special subsidies will also create an even playing field for all businesses instead of artificially picking winners and losers.

2.2.3 Move to a competitive territorial tax system. To bring the U.S. system more in line with our international trading partners', we recommend changing the way we tax foreign-source income by moving to a territorial system. Under such a system, income earned by foreign subsidiaries and branch operations (e.g., a foreign-owned company with a subsidiary operating in the United States) is exempt from their country's domestic corporate income tax. Therefore, under a territorial system, most or all of the foreign profits are not subject to domestic tax. The taxation of passive foreign-source income would not change. (It would continue to be taxed currently.)

As with the individual reforms, a number of details and transition rules will need to be worked out. However, the code should look similar to the following illustrative proposal:

Figure 9: Illustrative Corporate Tax Reform Plan

	Current Law	Illustrative Proposal (Fully Phased In)
Corporate Tax Rates	Multiple brackets, generally taxed at 35% for large corporations	One bracket: 28%
Domestic Production Deduction	Up to 9% deduction of Qualified Production Activities Income	Eliminated
Inventory Methods	Businesses may account for inventories under the Last In, First Out (LIFO) method of accounting	Eliminated with appropriate transition
General Business Credits	Over 30 tax credits	Eliminated
Other Tax Expenditures	Over 75 tax expenditures	Eliminated
Taxation of Active Foreign-source Income	Taxed when repatriated (deferral)	Territorial system
Taxation of Passive Foreign-source Income	Taxed currently under Subpart F	Maintain Current Law

RECOMMENDATION 2.3: PUT FAILSAFE IN PLACE TO ENSURE SWIFT PASSAGE OF TAX REFORM.

To ensure Congress moves quickly to enact comprehensive tax reform, the Commission recommends enacting a "failsafe" that will automatically trigger should Congress and the Administration not succeed in enacting legislation by 2013 that meets specified revenue targets. If Congress and the Administration do not act, the failsafe would impose either: 1) an across-the-board reduction of itemized deductions, above-the-line deductions, non-refundable credits for individuals, the income tax exclusion for employer-provided health care, general business credits, the domestic production activities deduction beginning in 2013 and increasing over time to raise $80 billion in FY 2015 and $180 billion in FY 2020; or 2) a trigger which reduced tax expenditures further and moved rates and expenditures down toward the levels specified in Recommendation 2.1, assuming such a trigger met the same revenue and progressivity targets.

III. Health Care Savings

Federal health care spending represents our single largest fiscal challenge over the long-run. As the baby boomers retire and overall health care costs continue to grow faster than the economy, federal health spending threatens to balloon. Under its extended-baseline scenario, CBO projects that federal health care spending for Medicare, Medicaid, the Children's Health Insurance Program (CHIP), and the health insurance exchange subsidies will grow from nearly 6 percent of GDP in 2010 to about 10 percent in 2035, and continue to grow thereafter.

These projections likely understate true amount, because they count on large phantom savings – from a scheduled 23 percent cut in Medicare physician payments that will never occur and from long-term care premiums in an unsustainable program (the Community Living Assistance Services and Supports Act, or "CLASS Act").

The Commission recommends first reforming both the formula for physician payments (known as the Sustainable Growth Rate or SGR) and the CLASS Act, and finding savings throughout the health care system to offset their costs. In addition, we recommend a number of other reforms to reduce federal health spending and slow the growth of health care costs more broadly.

Over the longer term (2020 and beyond), the Commission recommends setting targets for the total federal budgetary commitment to health care and requiring further structural reforms if federal health spending exceeds the program-specific and overall targets. We recognize that controlling federal health spending will be very difficult without reducing the growth of health care costs overall. To that end, the Commission's recommendations on tax reform regarding reducing and potentially eliminating the exclusion for employer-provided health insurance will help decrease growth in health care spending, according to virtually all health economists.

RECOMMENDATION 3.1: REFORM THE MEDICARE SUSTAINABLE GROWTH RATE.
Reform the Medicare Sustainable Growth Rate for physician payment and require the fix to be offset. *(Saves $3 billion in 2015, $26 billion through 2020, relative to a freeze)*

> The Sustainable Growth Rate (SGR) – known as the "doc fix" – was created in 1997 to control Medicare spending by setting payment targets for physician services and reducing payment updates if spending exceeded the targets. The SGR formula has required reductions in physician payments every year since 2002, but beginning in 2003 Congress blocked the reductions each year, requiring even larger reductions every subsequent year. Because of the accumulated shortfall from deferred reductions, the SGR formula would require a 23 percent reduction in 2012 payments, and will increase every year the problem is not fixed.
>
> Freezing physician payments from 2012 through 2020, as we assume in our baseline, would cost <u>$267 billion</u> relative to current law. The Commission believes that this amount – or the cost of any "doc fix" – must be fully offset, and recommends enforcing this principle by eliminating its exemption in statutory PAYGO. In the near term, we also recommend replacing the reductions scheduled under the current formula with a freeze through 2013 and a one percent cut in 2014.

For the medium term, the Commission recommends directing the Centers for Medicare and Medicaid Services (CMS) to develop an improved physician payment formula that encourages care coordination across multiple providers and settings and pays doctors based on quality instead of quantity of services. In order to maintain pressure to establish a new system and limit the costs of physician payments, the proposal would reinstate the SGR formula in 2015 (using 2014 spending as the base year) until CMS develops a revised physician payment system. The Medicare actuary would be required to certify the new payment system would not cost more than would have been allowed under the SGR formula.

This proposal would cost about $22 billion less than simply continuing to freeze physician payments, and therefore would reduce the deficit by that amount relative to our baseline.

RECOMMENDATION 3.2: REFORM OR REPEAL THE CLASS ACT.
(Costs $11 billion in 2015, $76 billion through 2020)

The Community Living Assistance Services and Supports (CLASS) Act established a voluntary long-term care insurance program enacted as part of the Affordable Care Act (ACA). The program attempts to address an important public policy concern – the need for non-institutional long-term care – but it is viewed by many experts as financially unsound. The program's earliest beneficiaries will pay modest premiums for only a few years and receive benefits many times larger, so that sustaining the system over time will require increasing premiums and reducing benefits to the point that the program is neither appealing to potential customers nor able to accomplish its stated function. Absent reform, the program is therefore likely to require large general revenue transfers or else collapse under its own weight, Commission advises the CLASS Act be reformed in a way that makes it credibly sustainable over the long term. To the extent this is not possible, we advise it be repealed. Technically, repealing the CLASS Act will increase the deficit over the next decade, because the program's premiums are collected up front and its benefits are not paid out for five years. To address this, we would replace the deficit reduction on paper from the CLASS Act with real options that truly save the federal government money and put it on a more sustainable path.

RECOMMENDATION 3.3: PAY FOR THE MEDICARE "DOC FIX" AND CLASS ACT REFORM. Enact specific health savings to offset the costs of the Sustainable Growth Rate (SGR) fix and the lost receipts from repealing or reforming the CLASS Act.

To offset the cost of the SGR fix and recover lost receipts in the first decade from repealing or reforming the CLASS Act, the Commission proposes a set of specific options for health savings that, combined, total nearly $400 billion from 2012 to 2020.

Medicare Savings

3.3.1 Increase government authority and funding to reduce Medicare fraud.
(Saves $1 billion in 2015, $9 billion through 2020)
The Commission recommends increasing the ability of CMS to combat waste, fraud, and abuse by providing the agency with additional statutory authority and increased resources (through a cap adjustment in the discretionary budget.)

3.3.2 Reform Medicare cost-sharing rules.
(Saves $10 billion in 2015, $110 billion through 2020)

Currently, Medicare beneficiaries must navigate a hodge-podge of premiums, deductibles, and copays that offer neither spending predictability nor protection from catastrophic financial risk. Because cost-sharing for most medical services is low, the benefit structure encourages over-utilization of health care. In place of the current structure, the Commission recommends establishing a single combined annual deductible of $550 for Part A (hospital) and Part B (medical care), along with 20 percent uniform coinsurance on health spending above the deductible. We would also provide catastrophic protection for seniors by reducing the coinsurance rate to 5 percent after costs exceed $5,500 and capping total cost sharing at $7,500.

3.3.3 Restrict first-dollar coverage in Medicare supplemental insurance.
(Medigap savings included in previous option. Additional savings total $4 billion in 2015, $38 billion through 2020.)

The ability of Medicare cost-sharing to control costs – either under current law or as proposed above – is limited by the purchase of supplemental private insurance plans (Medigap plans) that piggyback on Medicare. Medigap plans cover much of the cost-sharing that could otherwise constrain over-utilization of care and reduce overall spending. This option would prohibit Medigap plans from covering the first $500 of an enrollee's cost-sharing liabilities and limit coverage to 50 percent of the next $5,000 in Medicare cost-sharing. We also recommend similar treatment of TRICARE for Life, the Medigap policy for military retirees, which would save money both for that program and for Medicare, as well as similar treatment for federal retirees and for private employer-covered retirees.

3.3.4 Extend Medicaid drug rebate to dual eligibles in Part D.
(Saves $7 billion in 2015, $49 billion through 2020)

Drug companies are required to provide substantial rebates for prescription drugs purchased by Medicaid beneficiaries. We recommend extending these rebates to Medicaid beneficiaries who are also eligible for Medicare (individuals known as "dual eligibles") and who receive prescription drug coverage through the Medicare Part D program.

3.3.5 Reduce excess payments to hospitals for medical education.
(Saves $6 billion in 2015, $60 billion through 2020)

Medicare provides supplemental funding to hospitals with teaching programs for costs related to residents receiving graduate medical education (GME) and indirect costs (IME). The Commission recommends bringing these payments in line with the costs of medical education by limiting hospitals' direct GME payments to 120 percent of the national average salary paid to residents in 2010 and updated annually thereafter by chained CPI and by reducing the IME adjustment from 5.5 percent to 2.2 percent, which the Medicare Payment Advisory Commission has estimated would more accurately reflect indirect costs.

3.3.6 Cut Medicare payments for bad debts.
(Saves $3 billion in 2015, $23 billion through 2020)

Currently, Medicare reimburses hospitals and other providers for unpaid deductibles and copays owed by beneficiaries. We recommend gradually putting an end to this practice, which is not mirrored in the private sector.

3.3.7 Accelerate home health savings in ACA.
(Saves $2 billion in 2015, $9 billion through 2020)

The Affordable Care Act included several policies changing reimbursements for home health providers. The Commission recommends accelerating these changes to incorporate productivity adjustment beginning in 2013 and directing the Secretary of Health and Human Services (HHS) to phase in rebasing the home health prospective payment system by 2015 instead of 2017.

Medicaid Savings

3.3.8 Eliminate state gaming of Medicaid tax gimmick.
(Saves $5 billion in 2015, $44 billion through 2020)
Many states finance a portion of their Medicaid spending by imposing taxes on the very same health care providers who are paid by the Medicaid program, increasing payments to those providers by the same amount and then using that additional "spending" to increase their federal match. We recommend restricting and eventually eliminating this practice.

3.3.9 Place dual eligibles in Medicaid managed care.
(Saves $1 billion in 2015, $12 billion through 2020)
Approximately nine million low-income seniors and disabled individuals are covered by both Medicaid and Medicare. The divided coverage for dual eligibles results in poor coordination of care for this vulnerable population and higher costs to both federal and state governments. We recommend giving Medicaid full responsibility for providing health coverage to dual eligibles and requiring that they be enrolled in Medicaid managed care programs. Medicare would continue to pay its share of the costs, reimbursing Medicaid. Medicaid has a larger system of managed care than does Medicare, and this would result in better care coordination and administrative simplicity.

3.3.10 Reduce funding for Medicaid administrative costs.
(Saves $260 million in 2015, $2 billion through 2020)
We recommend asking states to take responsibility for more of Medicaid's administrative costs by eliminating Medicaid payments for administrative costs that are duplicative of funds originally included in the Temporary Assistance for Needy Families (TANF) block grants.

Other Savings

3.3.11 Allow expedited application for Medicaid waivers in well-qualified states.
In order to give states new flexibility to control costs and improve quality, we recommend increasing the availability of state Medicaid waivers. Specifically, we recommend establishing presumptive eligibility criteria for up to 10 states over the next decade. These eligible states would be required to proactively seek out the waiver and to meet certain objective threshold criteria, including: improved quality, efficiency, and cost of care; and not increasing the uninsured population. Applications would be evaluated and overseen by the Medicaid Center for Innovation.

3.3.12 Medical malpractice reform.
(Saves $2 billion in 2015, $17 billion through 2020)
Most experts agree that the current tort system in the United States leads to an increase in health care costs. This is true both because of direct costs – higher

malpractice insurance premiums – and indirect costs in the form of over-utilization of diagnostic and related services (sometimes referred to as "defensive medicine"). The Commission recommends an aggressive set of reforms to the tort system.

Among the policies pursued, the following should be included: 1) Modifying the "collateral source" rule to allow outside sources of income collected as a result of an injury (for example workers' compensation benefits or insurance benefits) to be considered in deciding awards; 2) Imposing a statute of limitations – perhaps one to three years – on medical malpractice lawsuits; 3) Replacing joint-and-several liability with a fair-share rule, under which a defendant in a lawsuit would be liable only for the percentage of the final award that was equal to his or her share of responsibility for the injury; 4) Creating specialized "health courts" for medical malpractice lawsuits; and 5) Allowing "safe haven" rules for providers who follow best practices of care.

Many members of the Commission also believe that we should impose statutory caps on punitive and non-economic damages, and we recommend that Congress consider this approach and evaluate its impact.

3.3.13 Pilot premium support through FEHB Program.
(Saves $2 billion in 2015, $18 billion through 2020)

The Commission recommends transforming the Federal Employees Health Benefits (FEHB) program into a defined contribution premium support plan that offers federal employees a fixed subsidy that grows by no more than GDP plus 1 percent each year. For federal retirees, this subsidy could be used to pay a portion of the Medicare premium. In addition to saving money, this has the added benefit of providing real-world experience with premium support.

Several Commissioners support transforming Medicare into a "premium support" system – such as one proposed by Representative Paul Ryan and Alice Rivlin – that offers seniors a fixed subsidy (adjusted by geographic area and by individual health risk) to purchase health coverage from competing insurers. A voucher or subsidy system holds significant promise of controlling costs, but also carries serious potential risks. To assess the balance of benefits and risks, we recommend a rigorous external review process to study the outcomes of the FEHB premium support program to determine its effects on costs, health care utilization, and health outcomes. Although the population covered by FEHB is different from the Medicare population, if this type of premium support model successfully holds down costs without hindering quality of care in FEHB program, that experience would be useful in considering a premium support program for Medicare.

RECOMMENDATION 3.4: AGGRESSIVELY IMPLEMENT AND EXPAND PAYMENT REFORM PILOTS. Direct CMS to design and begin implementation of Medicare payment reform pilots, demonstrations, and programs as rapidly as possible and allow successful programs to be expanded without further congressional action.

The Affordable Care Act requires CMS to conduct a variety of pilot and demonstration projects in Medicare to test delivery system reforms which have the potential to reduce costs without harming quality of care. These pilots include Accountable Care Organizations (ACOs), bundling for post-acute care services, and other programs to pay for performance. We recommend CMS be directed to aggressively pursue these and other reforms, including introduction of downside risk to ACOs and bundled payment pilots. CMS should also ensure that the private sector is an active partner in the research and design of payment reforms, building on concepts that have been proven to work at the state, regional, or federal level. In addition to Medicare pilots, we recommend that CMS be required to fast-track state Medicaid waivers that offer demonstrable promise in improving care and returning savings, such as Rhode Island's Global Consumer Choice Demonstration, which provides a capped federal allotment for Medicaid over five years; Vermont's all-payer advanced primary care practice reform, called Blueprint for Health; and Community Care of North Carolina, a provider-led medical home reform that has increased access to primary care, decreased emergency department usage, and saved money.

Pilots that succeed in controlling costs should be expanded as rapidly as is feasible. The Commission recommends shifting the presumption toward expanding reforms by requiring the Secretary to implement any pilot projects that have shown success in controlling costs without harming the quality of care by 2015. The Commission recommends utilizing the new Center for Medicare and Medicaid Innovation as the vehicle for accelerating these pilots. The Commission's plan does not assume any savings from expansion of these pilot projects in its deficit estimates, but believes that there could be substantial savings in Medicare, Medicaid, CHIP, and other health from aggressive implementation of successful pilots.

RECOMMENDATION 3.5: ELIMINATE PROVIDER CARVE-OUTS FROM IPAB. Give the Independent Payment Advisory Board (IPAB) authority to make recommendations regarding hospitals and other exempted providers.

The Affordable Care Act established the Independent Payment Advisory Board to recommend changes in Medicare payment policies if per-beneficiary Medicare spending grows too quickly. However, the law exempted certain provider groups, most notably hospitals, from any short-term changes from IPAB's authority. The Commission recommends eliminating these carve-outs.

RECOMMENDATION 3.6: ESTABLISH A LONG-TERM GLOBAL BUDGET FOR TOTAL HEALTH CARE SPENDING. Establish a global budget for total federal health care costs and limit the growth to GDP plus 1 percent.

Commission members, and virtually all budget experts, agree that the rapid growth of federal health care spending is the primary driver of long-term deficits. Some Commission members believe that the reforms enacted as part of ACA will "bend the curve" of health spending and control long-term cost growth. Other Commission members believe that the coverage expansions in the bill will fuel more rapid spending growth and that the Medicare savings are not sustainable. The Commission as a whole does not take a position on which view is correct, but we agree that Congress and the President must be vigilant in keeping health care spending under control and should take further actions if the growth in spending continues at current rates.

The Commission recommends setting up a process for reviewing total federal health care spending – including Medicare, Medicaid, the Children's Health Insurance Program, FEHB, TRICARE, the exchange subsidies, and the cost of the tax exclusion for health care – starting in 2020, with the target of holding growth to GDP plus 1 percent and requiring action by the President and Congress if growth exceeds the targets. This target should be adjusted to account for any changes in the health care exclusion enacted under tax reform. The target should be measured on a per-beneficiary basis if it is applied only to certain federal health programs, rather than globally. If health care costs continue to grow as fast as CBO and the Medicare actuaries project, or even faster as some Commission members believe will be the case, this process will require Congress and the President to consider further actions that make more substantial structural reforms. If the reforms in ACA are more successful in controlling costs than the estimates by CBO and the Medicare actuary suggest, as some Commission members believe, spending growth should be within the targets and this process would not be triggered.

We recommend requiring both the President and Congress to make recommendations whenever average cost growth has exceeded GDP plus 1 percent over the prior five years. To the extent health costs are projected to grow significantly faster than that pace, we recommend the consideration of structural reforms to the health care system. Commissioners have suggested various policy options, including: moving to a premium support system for Medicare; giving CMS authority to be a more active purchaser of health care services using coverage and reimbursement policy to encourage higher value services; expanding and strengthening the Independent Payment Advisory Board (IPAB) to allow it to make recommendations for cost-sharing and benefit design and to look beyond Medicare; adjusting the federal-state responsibility for Medicaid, such as block grants for acute or long-term care; establishing a robust public option in the health care exchanges; raising the Medicare retirement age; and moving toward some type of all-payer system.

Fostering an Economic Recovery

The Government Accountability Office has said that we could have double-digit growth for a decade and still not grow out of the current fiscal situation. At the same time, we cannot get out of this fiscal hole without sustained economic growth. According to the Office of Management and Budget, a one-time 1 percent decrease in GDP would increase the deficit by more than $600 billion over the course of the decade; if annual growth were 1 percent lower every year, the deficit would be over $3 trillion larger. A plan to reduce the deficit must therefore promote economic growth and not undermine the economic recovery. Our plan would accomplish these goals in at least four ways:

Reduce the deficit gradually. In order to avoid shocking the fragile economy, the Commission recommends waiting until 2012 to begin enacting programmatic spending cuts, and waiting until fiscal year 2013 before making large nominal cuts. In addition, revenue changes would not begin until calendar year 2013, after spending cuts are already well underway.

Put in place a credible plan to stabilize the debt. A number of economists have argued that putting into place a credible plan to reduce future deficits can have a positive effect on the economy. This so-called "announcement effect" could help to prevent interest rate increases and also mitigate uncertainty among individuals and businesses. In addition, stabilizing the debt will improve the country's long-term growth prospects by reducing the "crowd out" of private investment and by forestalling a potential fiscal crisis.

Consider a temporary payroll tax holiday in FY 2011. In order to spur short-term economic growth, the Domenici-Rivlin Bipartisan Policy Center Commission recommended a temporary payroll tax holiday in 2011. Assuming it is accompanied by sufficient future deficit reduction, Congress should consider a temporary suspension of one side of the Social Security payroll tax, financed by transfers from general revenue. Though this would cost $50-100 billion in lost revenue (depending on the design), CBO estimates that a payroll tax holiday of this magnitude would result in significant short-term economic growth and job creation.

Implement pro-growth tax and spending policies. In designing its proposal, the Commission made growth and competitiveness a priority. For example, our discretionary plan maintains important funding for education, infrastructure, and high-value R&D, and establishes a Cut-and-Invest Committee to continue to reprioritize spending toward investment. Our tax plan, meanwhile, cuts corporate and individual rates significantly, while simplifying the code, broadening the base, and lowering the deficit. It also makes us more globally competitive by moving to a territorial tax system like those of our international partners.

IV. Other Mandatory Policies

Slightly less than one-fifth of the federal budget is dedicated to other mandatory programs. These include civilian and military retirement, income support programs, veterans' benefits, agricultural subsidies, student loans, and others.

These mandatory programs are not projected to be the main drivers of rising deficits over the next ten years, but they nevertheless should be part of a comprehensive plan to correct our fiscal path. This is especially true because mandatory spending is not subject to the scrutiny of the annual appropriations process – so poorly directed spending can continue for years with minimal oversight. The Commission's goals in reforming these policies are:

> **Protect the disadvantaged.** About 20 percent of mandatory spending is devoted to income support programs for the most disadvantaged. These include programs such as unemployment compensation, food stamps, and Supplemental Security Income (SSI). These programs provide vital means of support for the disadvantaged, and this report does not recommend any fundamental policy changes to these programs.

> **End wasteful spending.** The first place to look for savings must be wasteful spending, including subsidies that are poorly targeted or create perverse incentives, and improper payments that can be eliminated through program integrity efforts.

> **Look to the private sector.** Some mandatory programs, like federal civilian and military retirement systems, are similar to programs in the private sector. When appropriate, we should apply innovations and cost-saving techniques from the private sector.

RECOMMENDATION 4.1: REVIEW AND REFORM FEDERAL WORKFORCE RETIREMENT PROGRAMS. Create a federal workforce entitlement task force to re-evaluate civil service and military health and retirement programs and recommend savings of $70 billion over ten years.

> Military and civilian pensions are both out of line with pension benefits available to the average worker in the private sector, and in some cases, out of line with each other across different categories of federal employment. The Commission recommends a federal workforce entitlement review to analyze civil service and military retirement programs in order to 1) Make program rules more consistent across similar programs, and 2) Bring both systems more in line with standard practices from the private sector. The review will have a ten-year savings target of $70 billion; recommendations of the task force would receive fast track consideration in Congress. Examples of program design reforms that the task force should consider include:

> > Use the highest five years of earnings to calculate civil service pension benefits for new retirees (CSRS and FERS), rather than the highest three years prescribed under current law, to bring the benefit calculation in line with the private sector standard. *(Saves $500 million in 2015, $5 billion through 2020)*

> > Defer Cost of Living Adjustment (COLA) for retirees in the current system until age 62, including for civilian and military retirees who retire well before a conventional retirement age. In place of annual increases, provide a one-time catch-up adjustment at age 62 to

increase the benefit to the amount that would have been payable had full COLAs been in effect.
(Saves $5 billion in 2015, $17 billion through 2020)

Adjust the ratio of employer/employee contributions to federal employee pension plans to equalize contributions.
(Saves $4 billion in 2015, $51 billion through 2020)

RECOMMENDATION 4.2: REDUCE AGRICULTURE PROGRAM SPENDING THROUGH 2020. Reduce net spending on mandatory agriculture programs by $10 billion from 2012 through 2020 with additional savings to fund an extension of the agriculture disaster fund, and allow the Agriculture Committees to reallocate funds as necessary according to their priorities in the upcoming Farm Bill.
(Saves $1 billion in 2015, $10 billion through 2020)

The Commission proposal recommends $15 billion in gross reductions in mandatory agriculture programs to achieve gross savings of $15 billion programs from FY 2012 to FY 2020, of which $10 billion will be dedicated to deficit reduction and $5 billion will be redirected to extending the Agriculture disaster fund program to mitigate the need for future ad hoc disaster funding.

The Commission recommends that the savings be drawn from across mandatory agriculture programs, including: reductions in direct payments when prices exceed the cost of production or other reductions in subsidies; limits on conservation programs such as the Conservation Stewardship Program (CSP) and Environmental Quality Incentive Program (EQIP); and reduced funding for the Market Access Program. The Agriculture Committees will be responsible for revising policies to meet their priorities in the upcoming Farm Bill within the lower baseline recommended by the Commission.

RECOMMENDATION 4.3: ELIMINATE IN-SCHOOL SUBSIDIES IN FEDERAL STUDENT LOAN PROGRAMS. Eliminate income-based subsidies for federal student loan borrowers and better target hardship relief for loan repayment.
(Saves $5 billion in 2015, $43 billion through 2020)

In light of recent legislation targeting student loan subsidies based on the income of the payer, the Commission proposes to eliminate in-school interest subsidies in federal student loan programs, which   Over the past several years, federal student loan policy has emphasized the principle of focusing student loans subsidies on reducing the burden of repayment and providing generous repayment protection. Targets subsidize student loans subsidies based on family income prior to the student's enrollment in college, rather than on the student's ability to pay after completion. According to a recent paper by The College Board, the most important consideration in enrollment decisions is how much the student will owe at the completion of studies, and there is no evidence that eliminating in-school interest is critical to that amount or to individual matriculation

RECOMMENDATION 4.4: GIVE PENSION BENEFIT GUARANTEE BOARD AUTHORITY TO INCREASE PREMIUMS.

The Pension Benefit Guarantee Corporation (PBGC) is a federal agency created to protect the pensions of participants and beneficiaries covered by private-sector defined-benefit plans. The PBGC is financed mainly through premiums assessed on employers offering defined benefit pension plans, as well as the assumed pension fund investments of failed companies; the agency receives no appropriations from general revenue. According to CBO and others, premiums are much lower than what a private financial institution would charge for insuring the same risk, but unlike private insurers (or even other similar agencies, such as the FDIC), the PBGC is unable to adjust the premiums it assesses from plan sponsors to cover potential liabilities. This has led to chronic and severe underfunding of the agency: as of the end of FY 2010, the PBGC's estimated liabilities exceeded its assets by $23 billion.

The Commission recommends allowing the PBGC's board to increase both flat- and variable-rate premiums (which are recorded in the budget as offsetting collections). Giving the PBGC board the authority to raise the premium rate to restore solvency and cover this shortfall will achieve mandatory budget savings in the near term, and more importantly, will sharply reduce the likelihood of a government rescue in the future.
(Saves $2 billion in 2015, $16 billion through 2020)

In addition to the options above, the Commission makes recommendations for a number of small programs. Savings are totaled; option descriptions follow.
(Saves $1 billion in 2015, $8 billion through 2020)

RECOMMENDATION 4.5: ELIMINATE PAYMENTS TO STATES FOR ABANDONED MINES.

The Abandoned Mine Land program at the Department of the Interior operates a fund for the reclamation of abandoned coal mines across the United States. The program is financed by a fee paid by the coal industry. In 2006, Congress authorized payments from the Abandoned Mine Land fund to states and tribes certified as having completed the reclamation of their abandoned coal mines – though payments can be used for any purpose. The Commission recommends eliminating these payments because they no longer serve their stated purpose -- contributing to reclaiming abandoned coal mines. Instead, they are paid to states and tribes whose mines have already been reclaimed.

RECOMMENDATION 4.6: EXTEND FCC SPECTRUM AUCTION AUTHORITY.

Since 1993, the Federal Communication Commission (FCC) has raised about $55 billion through its authority to assign radio spectrum licenses by competitive bidding. The Commission recommends that this authority, set to expire in 2012, should be made permanent. The Commission also encourages Congress to consider granting the FCC authority to conduct incentive auctions to free up spectrum for commercial wireless providers, which the FCC estimates could generate significant mandatory receipts.

RECOMMENDATION 4.7: INDEX MANDATORY USER FEES TO INFLATION.

The federal government charges user fees or licensing fees for a variety of products and services it provides to individuals and businesses. Where applicable, these fees should be indexed for inflation and should match market rates so that the burden of maintaining these programs is not shifted to taxpayers.

RECOMMENDATION 4.8: RESTRUCTURE THE POWER MARKETING ADMINISTRATIONS TO CHARGE MARKET RATES.

Power marketing administrations, part of the Department of Energy, generate and sell electricity from federally owned hydroelectric facilities and power plants. By statute, they are required to sell the electricity at cost. Raising prices to market rates would raise around $200 million in additional revenue each year.

RECOMMENDATION 4.9: REQUIRE TENNESSEE VALLEY AUTHORITY TO IMPOSE TRANSMISSION SURCHARGE.

The Tennessee Valley Authority (TVA) is a federally owned corporation that provides electricity to around 9 million people in the Southeast. TVA sells electricity below market rates, and its revenues are not sufficient to cover both its current operations and its debts. Adding a surcharge for all electricity transmitted by TVA would require TVA's customers – rather than American taxpayers at large – to cover TVA's costs.

RECOMMENDATION 4.10: GIVE POST OFFICE GREATER MANAGEMENT AUTONOMY

The Postal Service has run multi-billion dollar losses since 2007, and in 2010 maintained an operating deficit of $8.5 billion, even after receiving a $4 billion bailout from Congress the previous year. With the dramatic expansion of electronic mail, the volume of traditional air-mailed items will continue to fall, only worsening these enormous budget shortfalls and requiring even more federal funding in the future. To put the Postal Service on a path toward long-term solvency, the Commission recommends reversing restrictions that prevent the Postal Service from taking steps to survive – such as shifting to five-day delivery and gradually closing down post offices no longer able to sustain a positive cash-flow.

V. Social Security

Social Security is the foundation of economic security for millions of Americans. More than 50 million Americans – living in about one in four households – receive Social Security benefits, with about 70 percent going to retired workers and families, and the rest going to disabled workers and survivors of deceased workers. Social Security is far more than just a retirement program – it is the keystone of the American social safety net, and it must be protected.

Three quarters of a century after its creation, we must renew the promise of Social Security for the century ahead. When Franklin Roosevelt signed Social Security into law, average life expectancy was 64 and the earliest retirement age in Social Security was 65. Today, Americans on average live 14 years longer, retire three years earlier, and spend 20 years in retirement. In 1950, there were 16 workers per beneficiary; in 1960, there were 5 workers per beneficiary. Today, the ratio is 3:1 – and by 2025, there will be just 2.3 workers "paying in" per beneficiary.

Unless we act, these immense demographic changes will bring the Social Security program to its knees. Without action, the benefits currently pledged under Social Security are a promise we cannot keep. Today, the program is spending more on beneficiaries than it is collecting in revenue. Although the system's revenues and expenditures are expected to return to balance temporarily in 2012, it will begin running deficits again in 2015 if interest from the trust fund is excluded and in 2025 including interest payments. After that point, the system's trust fund will be drawn down until it is fully exhausted in 2037.

Unfortunately, the default plan in Washington is to do nothing. The do-nothing plan would lead to an immediate 22 percent across-the-board benefit cut for all current and future beneficiaries in 2037. Over the next 75 years, the program faces a shortfall equal to 1.92 percent of taxable payroll. Seventy-five years from now, that gap will increase to 4.12 percent of payroll.

The Commission proposes a balanced plan that eliminates the 75-year Social Security shortfall and puts the program on a sustainable path thereafter. To save Social Security for the long haul, all of us must do our part. The most fortunate will have to contribute the most, by taking lower benefits than scheduled and paying more in payroll taxes. Middle-income earners who are able to work will need to do so a little longer. At the same time, Social Security must do more to reduce poverty among the very poor and very old who need help the most.

Figure 10: Commission Social Security Plan and Present Law as Percent of Taxable Payroll

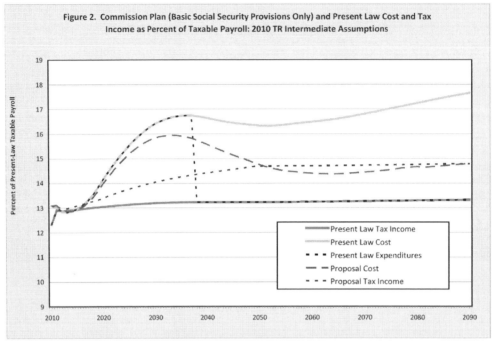

Figure 2. Commission Plan (Basic Social Security Provisions Only) and Present Law Cost and Tax Income as Percent of Taxable Payroll: 2010 TR Intermediate Assumptions

RECOMMENDATION 5.1: MAKE RETIREMENT BENEFIT FORMULA MORE PROGRESSIVE. Modify the current three-bracket formula to a more progressive four-bracket formula, with changes phased in slowly. Change the current bend point factors of 90%|32%|15% to 90%|30%|10%|5% by 2050, with the new bend point added at median lifetime income.

In order to control costs, the Commission proposes gradually moving to a more progressive benefit formula that slows future benefit growth, particularly for higher earners. Currently, initial benefits are calculated using a progressive three-bracket formula that offers individuals 90 percent of their first $9,000 of (wage-indexed) average lifetime income, 32 percent of their next $55,000, and 15 percent of their remaining income, up to the taxable maximum. The Commission recommends gradually transitioning to a four-bracket formula by breaking the middle bracket in two at the median income level ($38,000 in 2010, $63,000 in 2050), and then gradually changing the replacement rates from 90 percent, 32 percent, and 15 percent to 90 percent, 30 percent, 10 percent, and 5 percent.

Figure 11: Social Security Bend Points

Bend Point Locations in 2010	Current Law	Proposal	Projected Bend Point Locations in 2050 (in 2010 Dollars)
$0 to $9,000	90%	90%	$0 to $15,000
$9,000 to $38,000	32%	30%	$15,000 to $63,000
$38,000 to $64,000	32%	10%	$63,000 to $102,000
$64,000 to $107,000	15%	5%	$102,000 to $173,000
>$107,000	n/a	5%	$173,000 to tax max

Note: All numbers are FC staff estimated and rounded to the nearest $1000.

This benefit formula change will be phased in very slowly, beginning in 2017 and not fully phasing in until 2050. Because all bend point factors will continue to be *wage-indexed*, future beneficiaries will continue to have inflation-adjusted benefits larger than those received by equivalent beneficiaries today.

RECOMMENDATION 5.2: REDUCE POVERTY BY PROVIDING AN ENHANCED MINIMUM BENEFIT FOR LOW-WAGE WORKERS. Create a new special minimum benefit that provides full career workers with a benefit no less than 125 percent of the poverty line in 2017 and indexed to wages thereafter.

Social Security reform must ensure that the program can continue to meet its basic mission: to prevent people who can no longer work from falling into poverty. The Commission recommends creating a new special minimum benefit which provides full-career (30-year) minimum wage workers with a benefit equivalent to 125 percent of the poverty line in 2017 and wage-indexed thereafter. The minimum benefit would phase down proportionally for workers with less than 30 but more than 10 years of earnings.

RECOMMENDATION 5.3: ENHANCE BENEFITS FOR THE VERY OLD AND THE LONG-TIME DISABLED. Add a new "20-year benefit bump up" to protect those Social Security recipients who have potentially outlived their personal retirement resources.

The oldest old population – those over age 85 – is projected to expand rapidly over the coming decades: from 5.8 million this year to 19 million in 2050. To better insure against the risk of outliving one's own retirement resources, the Commission proposes a new "20-year benefit bump-up" that offers a benefit enhancement, equal to 5 percent of the average benefit, 20 years after eligibility. The enhancement is phased in over five years (1 percent per year). Eligibility is defined by the earliest eligibility age (EEA) for retirees and the determination of disability for disabled workers.

RECOMMENDATION 5.4: GRADUALLY INCREASE EARLY AND FULL RETIREMENT AGES, BASED ON INCREASES IN LIFE EXPECTANCY. After the Normal Retirement Age (NRA) reaches 67 in 2027 under current law, index both the NRA and Early Eligibility Age (EEA) to increases in life expectancy, effectively increasing the NRA to 68 by about 2050 and 69 by about 2075, and the EEA to 63 and 64 in lock step.

To account for increasing life expectancy, the Commission recommends indexing the retirement age to gains in longevity. The effect of this is roughly equivalent to adjusting the retirement ages by one month every two years after the NRA reaches age 67 under current law. At this pace, the NRA would reach 68 in about 2050, and 69 in about 2075; the Early Eligibility Age (EEA) would increase to 63 and 64 in step.

This approach would also maintain a constant ratio of years in retirement to years in adulthood; as life expectancy grows by one year, individuals will still be able to spend an additional 4 months in retirement, as compared to today.

RECOMMENDATION 5.5: GIVE RETIREES MORE FLEXIBILITY IN CLAIMING BENEFITS AND CREATE A HARDSHIP EXEMPTION FOR THOSE WHO CANNOT WORK BEYOND 62. Allow Social Security beneficiaries to collect half of their benefits as early as age 62, and the other half at a later age. Also, direct the Social Security Administration to design a

hardship exemption for those who cannot work past 62 but who do not qualify for disability benefits.

As workers approach retirement, they are faced with varying needs, and different retirement patterns make sense for different workers and their families. In recognition of these diverse experiences, the Commission's proposal introduces significant new flexibilities and protections in addition to an indexed retirement age.

First, the Commission proposes allowing beneficiaries to collect up to half of their benefits as early as age 62, with applicable actuarial reduction, and the other half at a later age (therefore incurring a smaller actuarial reduction). This increased flexibility should provide for a smoother transition for those interested in phased retirement, or for households where one member has retired and another continues to work.

Second, we propose a hardship exemption for those who may not qualify for disability benefits, but are physically unable to work beyond the current EEA. A recent RAND analysis reported that 19 percent of early retirees claimed a work-limiting health condition that would have limited their ability to continue in the paid labor force. To protect this population, the Commission proposal sets aside adequate resources to fund a hardship exemption for up to 20 percent of retirees. This exemption would allow beneficiaries to continue to claim benefits at age 62 as the EEA and NRA increase, and hold them harmless from additional actuarial reduction resulting from increased NRA. The Commission is charging the Social Security Administration with designing a policy over the next ten years that best targets the population for whom an increased EEA poses a real hardship, and considering relevant factors such as the physical demands of labor and lifetime earnings in developing eligibility criteria.

At the same time, the Commission recommends eliminating a provision that allows retirees who claim benefits early to withdraw a benefit application and return benefits received – even years after claiming – without paying interest or inflation, before reapplying for benefits at a later age and with a smaller actuarial reduction. This loophole is in effect an interest-free loan for wealthier retirees able to take advantage of it.

RECOMMENDATION 5.6: GRADUALLY INCREASE THE TAXABLE MAXIMUM TO COVER 90 PERCENT OF WAGES BY 2050.

As recently as the early 1980s, the Social Security payroll tax covered 90 percent of wages (in other words, 9 of every 10 dollars in wages were subject to the payroll tax). Since then, however, the taxable maximum wage cap (currently $106,800) has not grown as fast as wages above the cap; as a result, less than 86 percent of wages were subject to the payroll tax in 2009, and less than 83 percent will be subject to the tax by 2020. The Commission proposes to gradually increase the taxable maximum so that it covers 90 percent of wages by 2050. This recommendation would result in a taxable maximum of about $190,000 in 2020, versus approximately $168,000 in current law. The proposal will also de-link increases in the taxable maximum from increases in the Cost of Living Adjustment (COLA), allowing the taxable maximum to increase even in zero-COLA years.

RECOMMENDATION 5.7: ADOPT IMPROVED MEASURE OF CPI. Use the chained CPI, a more accurate measure of inflation, to calculate the Cost of Living Adjustment for Social Security beneficiaries.

As with the rest of the mandatory budget and the tax code, we recommend relying on the "chained CPI" to calculate the Cost of Living Adjustment (COLA) in Social Security, rather than the standard CPI. The Bureau of Labor Statistics has stated that the chained CPI is designed to more closely approximate a cost-of-living index than the standard CPI, and experts on both sides of the aisle have supported this technical improvement to the index.

RECOMMENDATION 5.8: COVER NEWLY HIRED STATE AND LOCAL WORKERS AFTER 2020. After 2020, mandate that all newly hired state and local workers be covered under Social Security, and require state and local pension plans to share data with Social Security.

Under current law, more than 90 percent of all workers are covered by Social Security, but a small share of states and localities exclude their employees from Social Security and instead maintain separate retirement systems. As states face a double hardship of prolonged fiscal challenges and an aging workforce, relying entirely on this pension model has become riskier for both government sponsors and for program participants, and a potential future bailout risk for the federal government. To mitigate this risk and to plan for an orderly transition to comprehensive Social Security coverage, the Commission proposes to mandate coverage for all state and local workers newly hired after 2020.

Full coverage will simplify retirement planning and benefit coordination for workers who spend part of their career working in state and local governments, and will ensure that all workers, regardless of employer, will retire with a secure and predictable benefit check. To improve the coordination of benefits for existing part-career state and local workers, the Commission also recommends requiring state and local pension plans to share data with Social Security.

RECOMMENDATION 5.9: DIRECT SSA TO BETTER INFORM FUTURE BENEFICIARIES ON RETIREMENT OPTIONS. Direct the Social Security Administration to improve information on retirement choices, better inform future beneficiaries on the financial implications of early retirement, and promote greater retirement savings.

Working longer and saving more has significant positive implications for both individuals and society as a whole. Yet the mixed signals sent to individuals often lead them to make less informed, and potentially precarious, choices. To help correct this, we propose directing SSA to provide better information to the public on the full implications of various retirement decisions, with an eye toward encouraging delayed retirement and enhanced levels of retirement savings. We encourage SSA to consider behavioral economics approaches (such as structured choice and others based in sound science) when providing this information.

Note that the Commission does not make specific recommendations to reform the Social Security Disability Insurance (DI) program or the Supplemental Security Insurance (SSI) program beyond program integrity investments discussed in recommendation 6.4. The Commission recommends a comprehensive redesign of the DI program to modernize both the program objectives and the eligibility criteria to better provide adequate and appropriate support to the disabled community without putting in place barriers to work and full community participation. This redesign is a critical next step, but is beyond the scope of this Commission.

RECOMMENDATION 5.10: BEGIN A BROAD DIALOGUE ON THE IMPORTANCE OF PERSONAL RETIREMENT SAVINGS.

Individuals need more financial assets and less debt, especially for retirement. Social Security forms the first tier of support for retirement but was never intended to be the sole source of retirement income. Retirement security solutions need to recognize and incorporate the challenges for self-reliant Americans who take responsibility for their families through a lifetime of work. Business owners and employees have historically negotiated over retirement benefits, and government employers face revenue challenges. Many private and public pension plans face serious underfunding of their long-term obligations.

A serious bipartisan conversation needs to take place regarding incentives to generate personal retirement savings that supplement Social Security and addresses the gap between what Americans need for retirement and what they currently have. Employers and employees can both play a role in strengthening the personal retirement savings of Americans. An ideal system should be open to all, portable, prevent leakage from high fees and early withdrawals and allow for pooled investments that can spread risk. It should encourage Americans to build wealth through savings and investment that will generate a return sufficient to allay fears that retirees will outlive their savings, and should permit Americans to have the option to transmit the remainder of their accumulated savings to their heirs. Americans need a fiscally responsible personal retirement savings system that is advanced funded, supplements the pay-as-you-go Social Security system, and accumulates funds for investments in business and infrastructure to help sustain a healthy economic growth rate.

Figure 12: Social Security Reform Provisions

	75 Year	75th Year
Gradually phase in progressive changes to benefit formula, modifying PIA factors to 90%|30%|10%|5% by 2050	45%	51%
Offer minimum benefit of 125% of poverty for an individual with 25 years of work; index minimum benefit level to wage growth	-8%	-6%
Index normal retirement age (NRA) and earliest eligibility age to longevity so that they grow about 1 month every two years. Also direct SSA to create "hardship exemption"	18%	30%
Provide benefit enhancement equal to 5% of the average benefits (spread out over 5 years) for individuals who have been eligible for benefits for 20 years	-8%	-6%
Gradually increase taxable maximum to cover 90% of earnings by 2050	35%	22%
Apply refined cost of living measure (chained-CPI) to COLA	26%	17%
Cover newly hired state and local workers after 2020	8%	0%
Add increased flexibility in retirement claiming options by allowing retirees to collect half of their benefits at a time, including by allowing them to collect the first half at age 62	-	-
SHARE OF EXISTING SHORTFALL CLOSED:	112%	102%

The plan proposed by the Commission is designed to restore actuarial balance as a stand-alone proposal. However, the tax reform process recommended by the Commission may separately result in additional payroll tax revenues into the Social Security system as a result of base broadening measures which would likely cause employers to shift some portion of non-wage compensation into wages (with resulting indirect increase in payroll tax revenues). As noted in the tax reform section, the Commission recommends that the precise details of tax reform be developed under a fast track procedure over the next two years. The impact of this reform on trust fund revenues will depend on the decisions Congress makes in the process. If Congress considers the Commission's Social Security recommendations in conjunction with or subsequent to tax reform legislation that results in additional trust fund revenue, this additional revenue will provide flexibility to moderate the changes in benefits or taxation recommended by the Commission.

Figure 13: Social Security Distributional Analysis

2050 Distribution (Including Illustrative Hardship Benefit)

	Average Annual Benefit			Mean Change in Benefits	
	Scheduled	Payable	Plan	Payable	Scheduled
Bottom Quintile	$9,732	$7,656	$10,284	31.9%	3.8%
2nd Quintile	$14,268	$11,208	$14,340	27.3%	0.0%
Middle Quintile	$18,000	$14,148	$16,488	16.2%	-8.7%
4th Quintile	$22,140	$17,400	$18,840	8.4%	-14.8%
Top Quintile	$27,480	$21,600	$22,416	3.4%	-18.7%

2070 Distribution (Including Illustrative Hardship Benefit)

	Average Annual Benefit			Mean Change in Benefits	
	Scheduled	Payable	Plan	Payable	Scheduled
Bottom Quintile	$12,300	$9,432	$12,708	33.8%	2.6%
2nd Quintile	$17,880	$13,716	$17,664	27.5%	-2.2%
Middle Quintile	$22,308	$17,100	$19,512	14.5%	-12.2%
4th Quintile	$27,612	$21,180	$21,336	4.2%	-20.1%
Top Quintile	$34,092	$26,148	$24,624	-3.8%	-26.2%

2050 Distribution (Excluding Hardship Benefit)

	Average Annual Benefit			Mean Change in Benefits	
	Scheduled	Payable	Plan	Payable	Scheduled
Bottom Quintile	$9,732	$7,656	$10,164	30.2%	2.4%
2nd Quintile	$14,268	$11,208	$13,872	23.2%	-3.2%
Middle Quintile	$18,000	$14,148	$16,344	14.0%	-10.4%
4th Quintile	$22,140	$17,400	$18,804	7.6%	-15.4%
Top Quintile	$27,480	$21,600	$22,416	3.1%	-19.0%

2070 Distribution (Excluding Hardship Benefit)

	Average Annual Benefit			Mean Change in Benefits	
	Scheduled	Payable	Plan	Payable	Scheduled
Bottom Quintile	$12,300	$9,432	$12,480	31.1%	0.5%
2nd Quintile	$17,880	$13,716	$16,884	21.8%	-6.6%
Middle Quintile	$22,308	$17,100	$19,236	11.5%	-14.5%
4th Quintile	$27,612	$21,180	$21,300	3.3%	-20.8%
Top Quintile	$34,092	$26,148	$24,624	-4.3%	-26.6%

VI. Process Reform

RECOMMENDATION 6.1: SWITCH TO A MORE ACCURATE MEASURE OF INFLATION FOR INDEXED PROVISIONS. Rely on chained CPI to index all CPI-linked provisions across government.

The Commission recommends adopting the "chain-weighted" Consumer Price Index for Urban Consumers (C-CPI-U) for all federal programs and tax provisions that currently rely on the CPI-U and CPI-W. The C-CPI-U is an alternative measure developed by the Bureau of Labor and Statistics that uses a technical improvement to more appropriately adjust for upper level substitution bias – one factor in how consumers change purchase decisions as relative market prices change. For example, when one product in the market basket (apples) becomes more expensive, consumers will forego purchasing that item in favor of a cheaper alternative (oranges).

RECOMMENDATION 6.2: ESTABLISH A DEBT STABILIZATION PROCESS TO ENFORCE DEFICIT REDUCTION TARGETS. Establish a debt stabilization process to provide a backstop to enforce savings and keep the federal budget on path to achieve long term targets.

The Commission proposal includes recommendations that would achieve enough savings to more than restore primary balance—that is, a federal budget balanced excluding interest payments on the debt—by 2015. Achieving primary balance for the budget would also stabilize the debt, meaning the debt would not grow as a percentage of GDP.

The Commission believes it is important for Congress and the President to remain vigilant to ensure the budget remains on a course to primary balance and a stable debt to GDP ratio. Previous budget enforcement mechanisms that placed limits on the deficit failed because they attempted to use budget process as a substitute for the tough choices needed to reduce the deficit. By contrast, this proposal provides a failsafe ensuring the fiscal goals envisioned by the Commission's recommendations actually materialize in the future.

The Commission recommends an enforcement mechanism to ensure the budget achieves primary balance by 2015 and the debt is stabilized thereafter. The Commission's proposal would require action by the President and Congress on budget stabilization legislation if the budget (excluding interest costs) is projected to have a deficit in 2015, or if the debt held by the public has not stabilized thereafter. The debt stabilization process would include fast-track procedures to facilitate changes in law necessary to protect the fiscal health of the federal budget.

The debt stabilization process recommended by the Fiscal Commission reflects a new standard for the President and the Congress to react in a timely manner to fiscal imbalance. Requiring the President to provide detailed legislative changes in law with his budget, coupled by the enactment of the Congressional budget resolution with directives to committees of jurisdiction to act by a date certain, will provide accountability and transparency to the federal budget process.

At the beginning of each year, OMB would report to the President and CBO would report to the Congress whether 1) the budget is projected to be in primary balance in 2015; 2) whether the debt held by the public as a percentage of GDP is projected to be stable at 2015 levels for the following five years; and 3) beginning in fiscal year 2016, whether the actual debt-to-GDP ratio will exceed the prior year's ratio.

In a year in which OMB indicates any one of these conditions has not been met, the President's budget would be required to include legislative recommendations that would restore primary balance in 2015 or, after 2015, stabilize the debt-to-GDP ratio.

If the Congressional budget resolution also shows that one of these conditions has not been met, the resolution would be required to include instructions for stabilization legislation to bring the budget back within the deficit or debt targets. This legislation would be considered under fast-track procedures similar to reconciliation. The legislation could include changes in law governing spending and/or taxes, including changes in discretionary spending limits. Discretion would be left to the committees of jurisdiction to determine the specific policies by which these goals are met. If Congress cannot agree upon a budget resolution in a timely manner, and CBO's report predicts one of these conditions has not been met, then any Member may introduce a stabilization bill, and a motion to proceed to that bill shall be considered on the floor of each House.

Congressional action on stabilization action would be enforced by a supermajority point of order against any legislation that would provide new mandatory budget authority or reduce revenues until a stabilization bill has been passed in years during which a budget resolution includes a stabilization instruction.

The stabilization process would be suspended if nominal GDP grew by less than one percent in the prior year. The process could also be suspended by the enactment of a joint resolution stating that stabilization legislation would cause or exacerbate an economic downturn.

Additional enforcement provisions to ensure Congressional action on stabilization legislation would strengthen this process. The Commission recommends Congress consider an automatic failsafe to keep the budget on course to meet these targets if future Congresses cannot agree on policies that achieve this result.

RECOMMENDATION 6.3: ALLOW CAP ADJUSTMENTS FOR PROGRAM INTEGRITY EFFORTS.

The Commission proposal includes cap adjustments to ensure appropriations are provided for Continuing Disability Reviews, Internal Revenue Service enforcement, and HHS and Department of Labor anti-fraud efforts (up to a specified amount).

RECOMMENDATION 6.4: REVIEW AND REFORM BUDGET CONCEPTS.

Current scoring rules and definitions cause policy makers to undervalue some policies and overvalue others. The Commission recommends a complete review of all budget scoring practices ("budget concepts") by the budget committees, the

Congressional Budget Office, and the Office of Management and Budget. Changes should aim to more accurately reflect the true cost of government liabilities, including by considering accrual accounting, risk-adjusted credit reforms, and similar concepts. In addition, the assessment should also include a review of current scorekeeping practices concerning program integrity savings and to what extent budgetary scoring practices should be updated to more accurately reflect savings from provisions designed to combat fraud and produce future savings. In addition, scoring agencies should review the possible benefit of providing secondary budget estimates to certain major legislation which more fully reflect their potential economic impact.

RECOMMENDATION 6.5: DESIGN EFFECTIVE AUTOMATIC TRIGGERS FOR EXTENDED UNEMPLOYMENT BENEFITS.

Under current law, extended unemployment benefits are triggered when unemployment in a state meets certain criteria. However, these criteria are poorly calibrated to the current economy, as evidenced by Congress's frequent decisions to intervene with legislation providing ad-hoc extensions. As a consequence of these inefficient on and off switches, extended benefits are often provided too late, turned off too quickly, applied too broadly, or provide too much stimulus after recovery has begun.

The Commission recommends putting into place a more precise trigger mechanism that will both turn on more quickly when unemployment levels exceed a threshold and are increasing, and remain on should unemployment levels remain elevated at levels above a set threshold. Similarly, benefits should automatically turn off when unemployment falls below the threshold level. A second tier trigger could automatically turn on and off second tier extend benefits only in hardest hit states.

Such a trigger would both ensure a reliable, timely intervention when needed, and would divorce key countercyclical programs from the political whims of Congress.

The Moment of Truth: Report of the National Commission on Fiscal Responsibility and Reform

Appendix

The Moment of Truth: Report of the National Commission on Fiscal Responsibility and Reform

Figure 14

Bridge from Current Law to Plausible Baseline

(Billions of dollars)

	2012	2013	2014	2015	2016	2017	2018	2019	2020	Total, 2012-2015	Total, 2012-2020
Deficit under CBO Current Law Baseline	-665	-525	-438	-507	-585	-579	-562	-634	-685	-2,136	-5,180
Policy Adjustments											
Enact Permanent "Doc Fix" (SGR)	-19	-22	-23	-25	-28	-31	-35	-40	-44	-90	-267
Renew 2001/2003 Tax Cuts Protected by Statutory PAYGO (on income below $200k/$250k)	-156	-144	-146	-147	-147	-146	-146	-147	-148	-593	-1,327
Continue Estate Tax at 2009 Levels	-34	-21	-23	-26	-28	-30	-31	-33	-34	-104	-260
Continue AMT Patches (including interactions)	-77	-88	-99	-110	-122	-136	-152	-169	-188	-373	-1,141
Adopt President's Discretionary Path (adjusted to	24	67	84	88	94	98	102	105	101	263	762
Assume Gradual Decline in OCO Troop Levels	-70	-68	-45	-17	-2	4	7	8	8	-200	-175
Subtotal, Policy Adjustments	-333	-277	-251	-237	-232	-242	-255	-276	-304	-1,098	-2,408
Net Interest	-6	-18	-33	-53	-72	-92	-113	-135	-146	-110	-669
Total Effect on the Deficit	-339	-295	-284	-290	-304	-334	-369	-411	-451	-1,208	-3,076
Total Deficit under Plausible Baseline	-1,004	-819	-722	-798	-889	-913	-931	-1,045	-1,136	-3,344	-8,257

Figure 15

Plausible Baseline

(Billions of dollars)	2010	2011	2012	2013	2014	2015	2016	2017	2018	2019	2020	2011-2015	2011-2020
Revenues													
Total	2,143	2,511	2,719	3,015	3,327	3,493	3,712	3,922	4,126	4,326	4,521	15,066	35,673
Outlays													
Social Security	701	726	753	789	831	878	931	989	1,052	1,119	1,191	3,978	9,259
Health Care	738	799	791	849	949	1,049	1,172	1,250	1,315	1,426	1,523	4,438	11,124
Other Mandatory	487	573	479	452	447	449	473	471	468	493	505	2,400	4,811
Discretionary	1,358	1,414	1,434	1,400	1,379	1,372	1,389	1,409	1,433	1,472	1,513	6,998	14,214
Net interest	202	226	265	344	444	545	636	715	788	860	938	1,824	5,762
Total	3,485	3,738	3,723	3,834	4,051	4,291	4,601	4,835	5,056	5,370	5,671	19,637	45,170
Deficit (-) or Surplus	-1,342	-1,227	-1,004	-819	-723	-798	-889	-913	-931	-1,044	-1,149	-4,571	-9,498
Debt Held by the Public	9,032	10,168	11,220	12,075	12,837	13,695	14,658	15,655	16,680	17,821	19,109	n.a.	n.a.

(Percent of GDP)	2010	2011	2012	2013	2014	2015	2016	2017	2018	2019	2020	2011-2015	2011-2020
Revenues													
Total	14.6%	16.6%	17.2%	18.1%	18.7%	18.8%	19.0%	19.2%	19.4%	19.5%	19.5%	18.8%	18.7%
Outlays													
Social Security	4.8%	4.8%	4.8%	4.7%	4.7%	4.7%	4.8%	4.8%	4.9%	5.0%	5.1%	5.0%	4.9%
Health Care	5.0%	5.3%	5.0%	5.1%	5.3%	5.6%	6.0%	6.1%	6.2%	6.4%	6.6%	5.5%	5.8%
Other Mandatory	3.3%	3.8%	3.0%	2.7%	2.5%	2.4%	2.4%	2.3%	2.2%	2.2%	2.2%	3.0%	2.5%
Discretionary	9.3%	9.3%	9.1%	8.4%	7.8%	7.4%	7.1%	6.9%	6.7%	6.6%	6.5%	8.7%	7.5%
Net interest	1.4%	1.5%	1.7%	2.1%	2.5%	2.9%	3.3%	3.5%	3.7%	3.9%	4.1%	2.3%	3.0%
Total	23.8%	24.7%	23.6%	23.0%	22.8%	23.0%	23.6%	23.7%	23.7%	24.2%	24.5%	24.5%	23.7%
Deficit (-) or Surplus	-9.1%	-8.1%	-6.4%	-4.9%	-4.1%	-4.3%	-4.6%	-4.5%	-4.4%	-4.7%	-5.0%	-5.7%	-5.0%
Debt Held by the Public	61.6%	67.1%	71.2%	72.3%	72.3%	73.5%	75.1%	76.7%	78.3%	80.3%	82.5%	n.a.	n.a.
Memorandum:													
Gross Domestic Product		14,666	15,148	15,764	16,705	17,760	18,630	19,508	20,398	21,293	22,205	23,154	80,044	190,567

Figure 16

Commission Plan

(Billions of dollars)

	2010	2011	2012	2013	2014	2015	2016	2017	2018	2019	2020	2011-2015	2011-2020
Revenues													
Total	2,143	2,511	2,722	3,045	3,387	3,603	3,844	4,077	4,303	4,541	4,774	15,268	36,806
Outlays													
Social Security	701	726	752	786	826	870	921	975	1,035	1,100	1,167	3,960	9,159
Health Care	738	799	795	828	917	1,013	1,133	1,208	1,261	1,367	1,461	4,353	10,782
Other Mandatory	487	573	475	441	433	429	449	443	435	456	463	2,351	4,596
Discretionary	1,358	1,379	1,385	1,297	1,237	1,200	1,195	1,195	1,197	1,210	1,222	6,498	12,518
Net interest	202	226	264	338	429	511	579	628	670	705	739	1,768	5,089
Total	3,485	3,703	3,671	3,691	3,842	4,024	4,276	4,450	4,597	4,839	5,052	18,930	42,144
Deficit (-) or Surplus	-1,342	-1,192	-949	-646	-455	-421	-432	-372	-294	-298	-279	-3,663	-5,338
Debt Held by the Public	9,031	10,133	11,200	11,952	12,497	13,004	13,522	13,987	14,380	14,779	15,164	n.a.	n.a.

(Percent of GDP)

	2010	2011	2012	2013	2014	2015	2016	2017	2018	2019	2020	2011-2015	2011-2020
Revenues													
Total	14.6%	16.6%	17.3%	18.2%	19.1%	19.3%	19.7%	20.0%	20.2%	20.5%	20.6%	19.1%	19.3%
Outlays													
Social Security	4.8%	4.8%	4.8%	4.7%	4.7%	4.7%	4.7%	4.8%	4.9%	5.0%	5.0%	4.9%	4.8%
Health Care	5.0%	5.3%	5.0%	5.0%	5.2%	5.4%	5.8%	5.9%	5.9%	6.2%	6.3%	5.4%	5.7%
Other Mandatory	3.3%	3.8%	3.0%	2.6%	2.4%	2.3%	2.3%	2.2%	2.0%	2.1%	2.0%	2.9%	2.4%
Discretionary	9.3%	9.1%	8.8%	7.8%	7.0%	6.4%	6.1%	5.9%	5.6%	5.5%	5.3%	8.1%	6.6%
Net interest	1.4%	1.5%	1.7%	2.0%	2.4%	2.7%	3.0%	3.1%	3.1%	3.2%	3.2%	2.2%	2.7%
Total	23.8%	24.4%	23.3%	22.1%	21.6%	21.6%	21.9%	21.8%	21.6%	21.8%	21.8%	23.6%	22.1%
Deficit (-) or Surplus	-9.15%	-7.9%	-6.0%	-3.9%	-2.6%	-2.3%	-2.2%	-1.8%	-1.4%	-1.3%	-1.2%	-4.6%	-2.8%
Debt Held by the Public	61.6%	66.9%	71.0%	71.5%	70.4%	69.8%	69.3%	68.6%	67.5%	66.6%	65.5%	n.a.	n.a.

Memorandum:

	2010	2011	2012	2013	2014	2015	2016	2017	2018	2019	2020	2011-2015	2011-2020
Gross Domestic Product	14,666	15,148	15,764	16,705	17,760	18,630	19,508	20,398	21,293	22,205	23,154	80,044	190,567

Figure 17

Effect of Commission Plan on Deficits

(Billions of dollars)	2012	2013	2014	2015	2016	2017	2018	2019	2020	Total, 2012-2015	Total, 2012-2020
Plausible Baseline	-1,004	-819	-723	-798	-889	-913	-931	-1,044	-1,149	-3,344	-8,270
General Revenues											
Comprehensive Tax Reform/Failsafe	0	20	40	80	90	105	120	150	180	140	785
Raise Gas Tax by 15 Cents	0	2	7	12	17	19	19	19	19	21	114
Apply Chained-CPI Throughout Government	1	3	4	6	10	13	17	20	23	13	96
Total Effect on General Revenues	1	24	51	98	117	137	156	189	223	174	996
General Outlays											
Discretionary Spending Caps	-49	-102	-141	-172	-194	-215	-236	-261	-291	-464	-1,661
Health Care Reforms											
Reform Sustainable Growth Rate	0	-2	-3	-3	-3	-3	-4	-4	-4	-8	-26
Reform or Repeal the CLASS Act	6	9	10	11	10	9	8	7	6	36	76
Require Rebate Payments from Drug Companies	0	-2	-6	-7	-6	-7	-7	-7	-7	-15	-49
Reduce Spending for Graduate Medical Education	0	-5	-6	-6	-8	-8	-8	-9	-10	-17	-60
Expand Medicare Cost Sharing, Restrict Medigap Coverage, and Create a Catastrophic Cap	0	-10	-10	-10	-10	-10	-20	-20	-20	-30	-110
Enact Tort Reform	-1	-1	-1	-2	-2	-2	-2	-3	-3	-5	-17
Restrict Medicaid Tax-Gaming	0	-2	-5	-5	-6	-6	-6	-7	-7	-12	-44
Reform TRICARE for Life to Align with Medigap Rules	0	-3	-4	-4	-5	-5	-5	-6	-6	-11	-38
Enact Premium Support Pilot for Federal Employees	0	-1	-2	-2	-2	-2	-3	-3	-3	-5	-18
Other Health Changes	-1	-4	-5	-7	-7	-7	-7	-7	-8	-18	-55
Other Mandatory Savings											
Apply Chained-CPI Throughout Government	-1	-1	-2	-3	-4	-6	-7	-9	-10	-7	-43
Reform Federal Civilian & Military Retirement	0	-1	-2	-5	-8	-11	-13	-15	-18	-8	-73
Reduce Farm Subsidies	0	-1	-1	-1	-1	-1	-1	-2	-2	-3	-10
Allow PBGC to Set its Own Premiums	0	-2	-2	-2	-2	-2	-2	-2	-2	-6	-16
Eliminate In-School Interest Subsidies for Student Loans	-3	-5	-5	-5	-5	-5	-5	-5	-5	-18	-43
Reduce Fraud (Program Integrity Adjustments)	0	-1	-1	-2	-3	-3	-4	-4	-4	-4	-22
Other Changes	-1	-1	-1	-1	-1	-1	-1	-1	-1	-3	-8
Total Effect on Outlays	-49	-135	-188	-227	-258	-284	-324	-358	-395	-599	-2,218
Social Security											
Revenue											
Gradually Raise Taxable Maximum to Cover 90% of Wages	3	5	8	12	14	18	22	26	30	28	138
Subtotal, Revenue	3	5	8	12	14	18	22	26	30	28	138
Benefits											
Chained-CPI	-1	-3	-5	-8	-10	-12	-14	-17	-19	-18	-89
Other Changes	0	0	0	0	0	-2	-2	-2	-5	0	-11
Subtotal, Benefits	-1	-3	-5	-8	-10	-14	-16	-19	-24	-18	-100
Total Deficit Effect of SS Reform	4	9	14	19	24	32	38	45	54	45	238
Net Interest	-1	-5	-16	-33	-58	-87	-119	-155	-199	-56	-673
Total Effect on the Deficit	56	173	268	377	457	540	636	747	871	874	4,125
Total Deficit under Commission Plan	-949	-646	-455	-421	-432	-372	-294	-298	-279	-2,471	-4,146

Made in the USA
Lexington, KY
02 October 2012